GOD'S Love LANGUAGE

GOD'S *Love* LANGUAGE
Why Do Bad Things Happen to Good People

DWIGHT TESKE

Xulon Press
2301 Lucien Way #415
Maitland, FL 32751
407.339.4217
www.xulonpress.com

© 2020 by Dwight Teske

All rights reserved solely by the author. The author guarantees all contents are original and do not infringe upon the legal rights of any other person or work. No part of this book may be reproduced in any form without the permission of the author. The views expressed in this book are not necessarily those of the publisher.

Unless otherwise indicated, Scripture quotations taken from the Holy Bible, New International Version (NIV). Copyright © 1973, 1978, 1984, 2011 by Biblica, Inc.™. Used by permission. All rights reserved.

Scripture quotations taken from the King James Version (KJV) – *public domain*.

Scripture quotations taken from the New American Standard Bible (NASB). Copyright © 1960, 1962, 1963, 1968, 1971, 1972, 1973, 1975, 1977, 1995 by The Lockman Foundation. Used by permission. All rights reserved.

Paperback ISBN-13: 978-1-6305-0938-5

Ebook ISBN-13: 978-1-6305-0939-2

TABLE OF CONTENTS

The Problem: Why Is There Suffering, Particularly Christian Suffering?..1
What Are We Trying to Accomplish?........................... 13
What Do We Expect?... 27
What Happens When We Do Not Get What We Expect?........ 33
Have You Ever Been Spiritually Stranded in the Desert?.......... 45
What Does God Think We Should Do?.........................61
What Is God's Planned Result?................................. 73
Epilogue 93

Chapter 1

THE PROBLEM: WHY IS THERE SUFFERING, PARTICULARLY CHRISTIAN SUFFERING?

In a survey, people were asked to state one question they would ask God if they could. Not surprisingly, the question they most frequently asked was, "Why is there suffering in the world?" It is a topic as old as recorded history.

I don't believe an adult exists who hasn't wondered about that subject at some time in their life. It is part of our mental process to try to make sense out of confusion or disaster, and unfortunately, we live in a world overflowing with disaster. The horror of incomprehensible terrorism, road rage, or shootings in a school, a church, a theatre, or some other public place fills the news.

Genocide occurs far too often in many third-world countries, this is not something we experience firsthand but the newsreel photos can be brutal. In first-world countries, our version of this comes out in hate crimes. We are not exempt from other tragedy. Too often, it's the boy next door who, to our utter shock and dismay, is exposed as a mass murderer. There are other equally horrific happenings that shock our sensibilities and when they do, one of the first questions asked by the news, the witnesses, and the survivors is *why*. "Why did this have to happen?" The remainder of the question, either stated or implied, is "If there is a God, why does He allow this to happen?"

GOD'S *Love* LANGUAGE

My own journey into this issue began a few years back. I'd grown bored in my retirement and began looking for something to do. I remembered something I'd read several years previously. It was a magazine article about Supercuts – the well-known hair salon. According to the article, many CPAs, financial advisors, business bankers, and others were getting into Supercuts because it showed a good return on the investment and was largely a hands-off business. Once established, the business required relatively little owner involvement.

I looked into it. I filled out an application, talked to both corporate Supercuts, and existing owners, and ran the numbers. I went so far as to fly from Southern California to Minneapolis, Minnesota, *in December*, to attend one of their introductory meetings. The success rate of their new franchises was extremely positive, so I decided to look into becoming a franchisee. My thought was I could be as involved as I wanted and have the potential of creating disposable income with the business profits to help others, something I had been trying to do for a good share of my adult life.

I love the wisdom of old Jewish men. As they say, "We plan, God laughs." God got a good chuckle on this one because Supercuts denied my application. Without going into the gory details, let me just say I went in a different direction with a brand-new concept designed to appeal to a previously ignored demographic, the upscale male population. The financials of this ground-floor opportunity looked fantastic, so I signed up.

Welcome to reality—God shut the door to a business opportunity with a greater than 90 percent rate of success and instead led me into a business with a nearly 100 percent rate of failure! While the concept looked good on paper, it did not work. In addition, the franchisor completely falsified all the financial documentation presented. So, then I found myself with a failing business on my hands, dumping money into it at an alarming rate, all the while being assured by the franchisor that it would turn around very soon. Needless to say, it did not.

The Problem: Why Is There Suffering, Particularly Christian Suffering?

While all this was going on, my morning, "God time" largely consisted of, *God, what in the world is happening? I went into this, at least in part, to help others. Helping others is a really big part of what I read in Your Word, but now, not only can I not help others, but I am watching my life savings go up in smoke.*

I can attest from firsthand experience that watching your retirement money disappear at age seventy-two can be a real test of your faith. In many ways, I failed the test miserably.

In addition to the financial issues that were tearing me up mentally, everything else in my life started falling apart. For example, I have a shed in my backyard that was built into a retaining wall. A mysterious water leak appeared that would flood that corner of my property with about two inches of water two to three times a week. That water began seeping into the shed through the block wall. I contacted the water department, and they sent someone out to investigate. After checking the meters on all the surrounding houses and finding no evidence of water leakage, the man gave up. His answer was, "I have no idea where the water is coming from, but it is not part of our system." Because neither he nor anyone else could explain where the water was coming from, I was forced to dig a trench around the side and back of the shed. That trench, at the rear, was six feet high.

So, at seventy-two years old and wiped out financially, I was using a pick and shovel to remove dirt so I could waterproof the block wall. A song at our church goes something like, "God is so good, God is so good, God is so good, He is good to me." As I was swinging the pick, I kept cadence by singing, "God is so mean God is so mean, God is so mean, He just hates my guts." At the time, I meant every word.

Within days of my completing this gruesome task, the mysterious water leak disappeared, never to come back, but then water started to seep into my family room. I cut an access panel in the kitchen's broom closet to see what was causing the leak and found a three-inch cast-iron drainpipe with a three-foot-long crack in it. I was forced to open up the wall to gain access. I removed the cracked section very carefully with a hand grinder, leaving a clean end to which I could attach a new piece of drainpipe. I then replaced the cracked section, repaired the wall, and repainted the kitchen.

I have a neighbor who grew up in construction. His father was a general contractor, and he has been a general contractor for the entirety of his adult life. When I shared my issues with him and showed him the cracked piece of cast iron drainpipe, his response was, "I have never seen anything like this in my life." This saga of problems continued for the next three years, almost without a break.

For example, at the time of this writing, I'd just completed a deposition arising from ongoing lawsuits over my failed business. I am suing the franchisor over the lies connected to the franchise, and in turn, I am being sued by the landlord over the lost rent on the business space, which I had personally guaranteed. The lawsuit against the franchisor was supposed to go to court first, which would likely have assigned the damages owed to the landlord to the franchisor. Unfortunately, the first case was postponed, so I face the possibility of losing the property that I'd put up for collateral. As we used to say when I was a kid, "The hits just keep on coming."

The lawsuits are now just a continuing reminder of all that happened, but while this was going on, I was still following my morning time with God, albeit grudgingly. That time consisted of reading five chapters from the Old Testament, five chapters from the New Testament, five psalms, and one chapter from Proverbs. I would come across verses like Proverbs 3:9–10: *"Honor the Lord with your wealth, with the first fruits of all your crops; then your barns will be filled to overflowing and your vats will brim over with new wine."* NIV. I would read that and think, God, *You are a liar. Not only are my barns not filled, but they have been struck by lightning and burned to the ground.*

Likewise, Malachi 3:10,
Bring the whole tithe into the storehouse, that there may be food in my house. Test me in this," says the Lord

The Problem: Why Is There Suffering, Particularly Christian Suffering?

Almighty, "and see if I will not throw open the floodgates of heaven and pour out so much blessing there will not be room enough to store it. NIV

To be perfectly honest, I kept tithing just so I could hold up my checkbook, look God straight in the eye, figuratively speaking, and say, "Okay, I answered Your challenge. Where are You?" I was mad and doing everything I could do to let God know how mad I was.

Through all this, I began meeting with my pastor on a semiregular basis. Brad has spent his own time in the spiritual tunnel, but that is his story to tell. Having been there, Brad did not offer much advice other than to encourage me to keep searching. He knew I needed to work out my own salvation, as Philippians 2:12 instructs. Sometime during this period, I gave up and quit going to church. My thought was, *Okay, God, let's strike a deal. I will leave You alone, and You give me the same consideration.* He didn't. Eventually, I reached the point where I was on my knees in the breakfast room praying, *God, if this is as good as it gets, just take me home.* I was tired and could not take it anymore. It is an interesting place when you cannot get any lower, and the only place left to look is up.

On top of all this, my wife developed stomach problems for which the doctors could not identify the cause or the cure. The headaches she had suffered from for most of her life, which had been under control, returned with a vengeance. Even her dog developed a liver and gallbladder infection that almost took its life. I spoke to Brad about this and in anger said, "It is one thing for God to mess with me, but why does he have to mess with my wife? His issue is with me, so leave her out of it!" A little clue to the last chapter, today Emilee, the dog who our vet at one point gave a 5% chance of survival, is in better shape physically and health-wise than she was before that almost fatal infection.

In situations like these, you reach the point where you can only cry out, "Where are You, God?" and "What possible purpose can there be for all of this?" In one of my conversations with Brad in a calmer frame of mind, I reflected that I did not understand the love of God. That I would never do to someone I loved what God had put me through. My logical mind understood that the bible states from cover to cover that God's love for us never fails but my emotional mind said how? The question I posed was "What exactly is God's love language"? Brads response was, I don't really know, someone needs to study that and write a book. If you don't maybe I will". That is where the question lay for about a year and a half until I realized that I would be given no peace until I started writing.

Mine is not a unique situation. I am a member of a Saturday-morning Bible study. Most of the members are experiencing their own issues, whether family health problems, financial difficulties, or any of the other usual problems everyone goes through from time to time—except, these problems seem to be enhanced, sort of like they're on steroids. I'll not say any more than that, as these sessions are confidential, but more than once I have heard someone say, "It seems like the harder I try to do right, the worse things get."

I had a friend, Kevin, who found Jesus while in his thirties. When Kevin found Jesus, he *really* found Jesus. Within a short period of time, his wife, who also had found Jesus, developed symptoms of multiple sclerosis. They both accepted her condition, even though within a relatively short time, she was wheelchair-bound. They continued to serve in whatever capacity they were able. Then, a little over a year ago, Kevin developed brain cancer and went from diagnosis to death in just over a year, leaving Marlene alone to cope with her MS. Everyone had expected Kevin to outlive Marlene, as he was the picture of health, but not so. The first question that most people would ask upon hearing this story is *why*.

If I'd spent the next month interviewing people on the street, I would be surprised to find even one person who did not have a personal story of tragedy or knows a friend with such a story. Sadly, there is an abundance of tragedy in the world. In America, we live with a relatively high standard of living, though some people do struggle. Even so, if you looked at third-world countries, you would be hard-pressed to

The Problem: Why Is There Suffering, Particularly Christian Suffering?

find anyone in America who is worse off than the poorest of the poor in these countries, where kids dig in garbage dumps to find something to eat. This assaults our senses in ways that are hard for us to process. It is our natural reaction to wonder why all this suffering occurs.

The problem is exacerbated for Christians because we have been programmed to believe that if we do right, we will be rewarded. As a result, we look at Christian suffering and question even more. In our minds, we justify the world's suffering, but we think it should be different for Christians.

In every society I am aware of on the face of this planet it seems that parents are instinctively aware that children need guidance from the moment they are born to ultimately live successful lives in their society. Many of those parents include spiritual guidance also. That spiritual guidance generally boils down to "there is a god of some kind somewhere that is watching also". I cannot speak for any other religion involved but having been raised in a Christian home I can speak to the fact that the knowledge about God has been present with me from my earliest recollection. That knowledge has in varying degrees been in my mind whatever I was doing. Speaking in general terms, in all probability, from the minute you were born in one way or another you were programmed to "behave." If you did wrong, you would be punished, and if you did right, you would be rewarded. Admittedly, the parental form of punishment and reward covers an extremely broad spectrum, but from the most lenient parent to the strictest, there is a punishment-and-reward system that almost every child grows up under.

Our school years are focused on punishment and reward also. If we work hard and study, we will get good grades. If we get into trouble, we will be sent to the principal. This same concept carries over into our adult lives. We get a job, and if we are diligent and work hard, we might get a promotion or a raise. Our whole lives are centered on a punishment-and-reward system. There are notable exceptions to this general premise, but for most of us, this is an accurate representation of how we live our lives.

The Bible speaks to this. As we read the Old Testament, we see how God's system of dealing with the Israelites was largely based on punishment and reward. In the books of Kings and Chronicles, the kings who did right and honored God were rewarded, while the kings who did wrong (created and worshipped false gods) were punished. There were, of course, some notable exceptions. Solomon, for example, married many foreign women – in direct contradiction to God's command. However, for the sake of his father, David, God did not take the kingdom from Solomon, though He did take it from Solomon's son. In another example, Moses was not allowed to enter the Promised Land because of one mistake. And on go the examples of how God handled His children's behavior.

Nonetheless, except for the occasional exception, the rule was, "Do good and prosper, but do wrong and suffer." Proverbs 3:9–10 and Malachi 3:10 seem to advocate that we should give to receive. There are entire ministries devoted to the "give to get" premise, but reality pops up when we see devoted Christians who are giving of their time and money but are barely scraping by.

Frank Pastore was a baseball player who was saved and became a popular talk show host on a local Christian radio station after his baseball career was over. His show was gaining listeners, and his Christian influence was growing, but then he was killed in a motorcycle accident. It is hard not to ask *why*. There are countless stories of missionaries who die on the mission field, and other stories where missionaries were protected from unbelievable situations. Again, *why*? Stories abound about devoted Christians, both laypeople and pastors, who suffer terrible tragedies. In our minds, we wonder, *"These are good, dedicated Christians who are giving their lives to promote the gospel, so... why are they suffering to such an extent?"*

It is not at all difficult to find good Christian people who suffer similar problems with completely different outcomes. Cancer is a good example; one person experiences a miraculous recovery while the next person dies. This upsets our sensibilities because we all, in varying

The Problem: Why Is There Suffering, Particularly Christian Suffering?

degrees, cling to the idea that if we do good, we will be rewarded, and if we do bad, we will be punished.

Read the book of Job. Job was diligent to the point of obsession about offering sacrifices for himself and his children, just in case they might have done something wrong. In Job chapter 1, we read that when his sons would hold feasts in their homes and the period of feasting had run its course, Job would make arrangements for them to be purified. Then, early in the morning, he would sacrifice a burnt offering for each of them, just in case they had sinned.

On one occasion, the angels presented themselves to God, and Satan was with them. God and Satan had a heavenly discussion about how diligent and faithful Job was. Satan challenged God, stating, "Why shouldn't Job worship You? Look at how rich You have made him." In response, God allowed Satan to attack all Job had and, in one day, Job was wiped out financially, and his children were all killed. To Job's credit, his reaction was, "Naked I came into this world, and naked I will leave. Blessed be the name of the Lord."

Then Satan was allowed to attack Job's health. As Job sat scraping his boils with a broken piece of pottery, his friends showed up to *comfort* him. His three friends, who were obviously from a very strict fundamentalist, legalistic denomination, began hammering Job with the idea that he must have done something wrong. Otherwise, God would not be doing these terrible things to him. Even his wife said to him, "Curse God and die." Job's response to her was, "Shall we accept good from God and not trouble?"

When Job's friends first arrived on the scene, they were so shocked at Job's appearance and the depth of his suffering that they began to weep. Initially, they all sat silently for a period of time, until Job began to speak. Obviously, Job had been anticipating sympathy from his friends, because he began to curse his birth, bemoaning the day he was born and wishing he had been stillborn so he would not have to endure the suffering. Then Eliphaz began to chastise Job by saying, *"Who, being innocent, has ever perished? Where were the upright ever destroyed? As I have observed, those who plow evil and those who sow trouble reap it," Job 4: 7-8 NIV.* His obvious implication was if Job had done nothing wrong, this trouble would not have come upon him.

>Job's answer was,
>*Teach me and I will be quiet; show me where I have been wrong. How painful are honest words! But what do your arguments prove? Do you mean to correct what I say, and treat my desperate words as wind? You would even cast lots for the fatherless and barter away your friend. But now be so kind as to look at me. Would I lie to your face? Relent, do not be unjust; reconsider, for my integrity is at stake. Is there any wickedness on my lips? can my mouth not discern malice?" Job 6: 24-30 NIV.*

Job also questioned God, "If I have sinned, what I have done to you, you who sees everything we do? Why have you made me your target? Have I become a burden to you? Why do You not pardon my offenses and forgive my sins?" Job 7:20-21 NIV.

Then Bildad replied, "How long will you say such things? Your words are a blustering wind. Does God pervert justice? Does the almighty pervert justice? When your children sinned against Him, he gave them over to the penalty of their sin." Job 8:2-4 NIV.

This discussion goes on for about thirty chapters, but I believe you get the point. And, if we will be honest with ourselves, we all will, at some point in a similar circumstance, wonder what that person did to deserve it, whatever *it* is.

Most Bible scholars agree that Job was probably a contemporary of Abraham, and that the book of Job was probably the first book written in what ultimately became the Holy Bible. So, the belief that good is rewarded and evil punished has been around since the beginning of recorded history.

The Problem: Why Is There Suffering, Particularly Christian Suffering?

The questioning of the secular world is similar. They, too, look at appearances and question why bad things happen to good people. Almost nightly on the news in the Los Angeles area, some tragedy occurs. Some innocent person gets caught in a gang shooting, and the reactions are always about how good and kind this person was. Or perhaps the victim is an innocent child, and the question is *Why this could happen to such a blameless person?* There is never a mention of any gang member who might have been killed in the same shooting, because the thought is they were not a good person and therefore they got what they deserved.

When someone gets hurt or killed in a crosswalk by a hit-and-run driver, it seems the victim is always a good, loving person, and the driver is a horrible, evil person. I am not saying there is no justification for this line of thinking. The only point I am making is that the Christian world and the secular world see things in much the same light. We have trouble understanding why bad things happen to good people.

There is also the issue of good things happening to bad people. A dishonest businessperson might succeed while an honest businessperson fails. Our mental thoughts, which have been programmed to believe that the good person should be rewarded, are turned upside down. We internally, if not vocally, cry, *this is not right and should not be.*

In Psalm 73, Asaph laments:

> Surely God is good to Israel, to those who are pure in heart. But as for me my feet had almost slipped; I had nearly lost my foothold. For I envied the arrogant when I saw the prosperity of the wicked. They have no struggles; their bodies are healthy and strong. They are free from common human burdens; they are not plagued by human ills. Therefore pride is their necklace; they clothe themselves with violence. From their callous hearts comes iniquity; their evil imaginations have no

limits. They scoff, and speak with malice; with arrogance they threaten oppression. Their mouths lay claim to heaven, and their tongues take possession of the earth. Therefore their people turn to them and drink up waters in abundance. They say, "How would God know? Does the Most High know anything?" This is what the wicked are like—always free of care, they go on amassing wealth. Surely in vain I have kept my heart pure and have washed my hands in innocence. All day long I have been afflicted, and every morning brings new punishments. Psalms 73:1-14 NIV.

Have you ever felt like Asaph? Have you ever looked at your situation and wondered, *where are You, God?* Have you spent your life trying to live right, while watching other people cheat in every way and succeed in everything they do? Welcome to the club. I suggest you read the thirty-first chapter of Job and see if you can relate to his conversation with God.

I grew up with an overdeveloped sense of justice, and I carry it to this day. I used to lament to my mother whenever someone cheated and won a game, and my mother would always respond, "Cheaters never prosper." That's another lie I will need to discuss with her when I see her in heaven.

I don't believe anyone on earth can truthfully deny a battle is raging between good and evil, and that too often evil is winning. Stick around till the last chapter, and I might challenge that premise, but no cheating and reading the last chapter first, because there is a lot of territory to cover before we get there.

Chapter 2
WHAT ARE WE TRYING TO ACCOMPLISH?

You are likely familiar with the parable of the sower. In this story, the sower threw seed on a prepared field, but some seed fell on the path. The path was hard and compacted from the countless people who had walked on it. Since the soil had not been broken up, the seed could not fall into it as it could on a plowed and prepared field. Consequently, as it lay on top of the compacted path, the birds grabbed it, and it was gone.

Some of the seed fell on rocky places. If you have ever been to Israel, you have noticed the abundance of stones everywhere. It is no wonder they used to stone people – the ammunition is everywhere. It is not difficult to imagine that a farmer, in preparing a field for planting, would have to first gather the stones and pile them on the edge of the field. As he scattered the seed, some was bound to fall on the stone pile. The rain would fall on these stones as it did on the field, and the seed would respond to the water and initially spring up. However, the water would soon evaporate, not having any soil to hold it in place, and the plant would wither and die.

Other seed fell in among the weeds that undoubtedly grew up at the edge of the rock pile. Anyone who has ever had a garden knows how hearty and tenacious weeds can be. They grow fast, grabbing every available spot of soil, and a plant that is arguing with a weed for a patch of soil is in for the fight of its life.

Finally, some seed fell on the good soil, the soil that had been plowed and properly prepared. This seed was able to put down roots to access the water and nutrients needed to grow to maturity and produce a crop.

This is a familiar parable, but I have a little different take on it than anything else I have ever heard. Let me share it with you.

First is the seed on the pathway. When the seed falls on an unprepared heart, the hearer does not understand the message. Satan will not let that seed remain and possibly, at a later date, take root. He will immediately inject some thought into that mind to take the seed away, thus preventing it from accomplishing anything useful. No discussion is necessary about these kinds of hearers—they did not even begin to understand and remained untouched by the seed that came their way.

The seed that fell on the rocky place represents hearers who receive the word with joy, but when trouble or persecution comes, they fall away because they have no root. Here is where I disagree with every sermon or teaching, I have heard on this parable. In every case, the speaker has stated that, even though this seed sprang up, it obviously did not result in salvation. However, in John 1:11–12, we read, *"He came to his own and his own received him not. But to all who received him [past tense], he gave the right to become [future tense] the children of God."*

The way I read this, the salvation that comes from accepting Jesus as your Savior and becoming a child of God are not synonymous.

The initial salvation is a first step, a fire insurance policy, so to speak. In 1 Corinthians 3, beginning with verse 10, Paul speaks about laying a foundation for others to build on. Believers have the choice to build with gold, silver, and costly stones, or with wood, hay, and stubble. At the final judgment, our work will be tried by fire. If what we built survives the fire, we will receive a reward; but if it is burned up in the fire, we will suffer loss, though we ourselves *will be saved* as one escaping through the flames. What Paul is referring to is the initial foundation Paul laid when he introduced someone to Jesus. When that person understood that Jesus' death, burial, and resurrection paid for all the sin they had committed, and they accepted that gift, they were saved and on their way to heaven. There is a second "salvation," that is what we do once we have received the first "salvation." That salvation is an eternal reward for our obedience in serving God with our time and possessions. Building with "gold, silver, and costly stones" is a figurative way of saying that everything done in grateful obedience to God will be part of the reward we will receive in heaven.

More on eternal reward later, but for now, it is critical that the reader understands that the first and second salvations are two separate and distinct actions. While the second is dependent on the first, the first is not dependent on the second. It is salvation and *then works,* not salvation by works.

The reference of being tried by fire is to the refining of precious metal. Ore is placed into a container that can withstand the heat of refining fire. The ore melts and the precious metal sinks to the bottom, as precious metals are heavy. The impurities float to the top and are skimmed off, leaving the pure gold or silver in the bottom of the container. Now let's put some wood, hay, or stubble into the refining container over a fire capable of melting ore and see how well it withstands the fire.

If you receive Jesus, you have a vehicle in which you can travel toward an adult Christian status, but it does not guarantee you will reach it. Once you accept Jesus, you are on your way to heaven, even if you never do another thing for the cause of Christ. In this case, having heard the gospel, you accept it and embrace it, springing up to spiritual life. But because of your circumstances – where you are in your life, the family you live in, the people you are accustomed to living with, or any number of other situations – you may find yourself in a place that is not conducive to growth, and your initial growth spurt shrivels and dies. Yes, Paul knew what he was talking about. This can happen.

The seed that falls into the weeds springs up, and because it is in soil somewhat conducive to growth, it manages to stay alive. However, it spends so much time fighting with the weeds, trying to gather the moisture and nutrients it needs to survive, it never reaches the point of producing the fruit that it could.

The seed that falls into the good ground grows to maturity and produces fruit.

This is a great mental picture, but what does it mean to us? Which category are you in?

Are you in category one? Maybe you have heard the gospel many times but are saying to yourself, *What does that mean to me?* Possibly, you are thinking, *I am basically a good person. I try to treat everyone the way I would like to be treated. I give to charity and try my best to do as much good as possible. I make every effort to make amends for the mistakes I inevitably make, but I am only human, and we all make mistakes. I believe that my good far outweighs my mistakes.* The problem with that line of reasoning is we cannot apply human logic to God. Since God made everything in the entire universe, in essence, He invented the game and built the playing field, so He can make whatever rules He wants.

I am in no way trying to be irreverent. The point I am trying to make is that by utilizing human logic, you are missing the most important event in the entire universe. The book of Hebrews, in the first chapter, clearly states that Jesus, the Son of God, was the creator of the universe. From the first day of creation to the last, Jesus did it all while God the Father and God the Holy Spirit looked on. However, the creation of man was so special that all three had a hand in it. Genesis 1:26 states, "Let *us* make man in *our* image" (emphasis added). The *us* refers to God in His three forms: Father, Son, and Holy Spirit.

And what did God do for this very special creation of His? He sent Jesus to earth to become a man. Jesus left heaven, relinquishing His right to divinity, and was born as any other child is born. However, His birth was special because His mother, Mary, was a virgin when she conceived Him by the power of God the Holy Spirit. Jesus grew up in a humble home with Joseph, His earthly father, and His mother, Mary. Joseph was a carpenter, so Jesus took up that trade while He was growing up.

At this point, it is necessary to understand something about the mind of God the Father. You do not need to spend a lot of time in scripture to realize that God looks at disobedience in the same way as a spouse looks at adultery. Beyond any other awful thing you can do to a spouse, unfaithfulness is at the very top of the list. There is nothing you can do to *undo* an affair. If you read through Jeremiah, Ezekiel and Hosea, God equates their disobedience with adultery. If you are trying to outweigh your bad with good behavior, it is a losing battle.

At the approximate age of thirty, Jesus began his ministry and traveled around, preparing the populace for the new covenant that would initiate in about three years. At the approximate age of thirty-three, He was crucified, died, and was buried. Three days later, he came out of the tomb, alive and well. Why did He do this? To answer that question, we need to go back to the Garden of Eden.

We all know about Adam and Eve eating the forbidden fruit. Because they ate that fruit, they were kicked out of the garden. You might ask why they would get kicked out and separated from God for eating a piece of fruit. The answer is simply that God said, *don't do it*. God is perfect and cannot be in the presence of imperfection, so that one mistake cost them the right to live in the garden and walk and talk with God. If you were to somehow live an absolutely perfect life, with only one exception – one little curse word, one little lie, or one little whatever – you still could not be in the presence of God, Adam and Eve just had a piece of fruit, but that piece of fruit was disobedience to God. It actually gets worse! James in his letter chapter 4 v17 states that if someone knows to do good and does not do it, for them that is sin. God's standard is so high that you do not need to do something wrong but not doing something right is enough to condemn you.

By now some of you are probably wondering okay, what is this all about? God created man because He wanted a creation to interact with. God wanted someone to love and someone to love Him in return, and that creation was man. God's only request was that man love Him enough not to eat the forbidden fruit. Man blew it and spurned God's love. To reestablish that love connection, Jesus came to earth as a man – a man who lived a perfect life and then offered Himself as a sacrifice acceptable to God. For the sins of the whole world, He was willing to die on a Roman cross, probably the most horrific form of capital punishment man has ever come up with. He did that for me, and He did that for you. God could have forced Adam and Eve to obey, but forced obedience is not love.

God the Father cannot interact with a sinful creature, and we as sinful creatures cannot even begin understand the idea of a perfect God. Jesus, on the other hand, was born as any other baby. He grew up as any other child, with the exception that, even though He was tempted as all children are, He never yielded to temptation; never once did Jesus sin in any way. Regardless of the fact that He was perfect, He still understands the temptation of sin and how it can pull at us until we give in. The point is Jesus, having lived as a human being in an imperfect world, understands us. Inversely, having spent eternity past with God the Father and God the Holy Spirit, He understands a perfect God. He is able to bridge that gap and assist both sides to communicate with the other.

In every real sense, Jesus is both perfect God and perfect man in the same package. Let's dig into this concept a little bit. Our natural inclination is to think, *Hey it was just a piece of fruit!* The issue is not what it was or how insignificant we may think it to be, to an absolutely holy God it was disobedience. We have already compared disobedience with adultery, so our opinion does not matter only our actions. On the other side of that coin, we have our sin. God cannot look at us without seeing our sin. However, if God looks at us through the filter of Jesus' sacrifice on the cross, paying the price for our sin, He no longer sees the sin because Jesus has filtered it out of the picture. This *only* applies *after* we have received Jesus as our savior. I suggest that you stop for a moment and let the emphasis of that statement sink in.

I have spent a lot of space on you in group one because you need to understand this, but I am not done. There is another dynamic in group one. There are people out there who believe they have done so much wrong they are beyond hope. The truth is no one is so bad they cannot be forgiven.

What Are We Trying To Accomplish?

Let me tell you a story. There was once a religious zealot who lived in a part of the world that did not offer the personal protections we enjoy in this country. He used to travel around finding Christians and throwing them into jail. On one occasion, a mob was killing a Christian and he was rooting them on as he held their coats. His religious sect supported him in everything he did. They supplied support and traveling companions as he moved through the countryside looking for Christians he could have jailed or even killed. Living to persecute Christians in any way he could became his reason for existence.

One day this man came face-to-face with Jesus. He had to face the fact that the way he was living was completely wrong, and he became a missionary. We now know this man as the apostle Paul, the man who probably did more to establish the first-century church than any other person, and the one who wrote over half of the New Testament.

I do not know who you are or what your story is, but your life probably is no worse than Paul's. And even if it is worse, God can still forgive you if you ask.

A third segment of group one is composed of those who are entirely self-sufficient. They have been successful in everything they have done and enjoy health, wealth, and happiness... or do they? Most people I have encountered in this group are never satisfied, always striving for something more and the next hill to conquer. John D. Rockefeller Sr., one of the richest men of his era, was once asked what was enough. His answer was, "Just a little more." Just a little more money, just a little fancier car, just a little bigger house, just a little bit more... of everything.

The Bible expresses its view on this in Mark 8:36. "What does it profit a man to gain the whole world and lose his own soul?" Imagine for a minute a string stretched from the earth to the outer reaches of the universe. Now let's put a small dot somewhere on that string. That dot, in relation to the string, represents your lifetime in relation to eternity. Why would anyone choose to possess everything for the time represented by that dot and spend the rest of eternity in eternal punishment,

GOD'S *Love* LANGUAGE

or without any reward? There are many references in the Bible stating eternal punishment is just that, for eternity.

Other people depend on education. They reason that science disproves the existence of God, that creation just happened, and somehow life came into existence. Life evolved over millions of years, and God had nothing to do with it, they claim. The problem is science changes its mind every few years as new things are discovered. Think of the big bang theory. I do not remember how long-ago science came up with that, but even Stephen Hawking would not go one millisecond before the alleged *big bang* to try to explain the uncaused first cause. All the laws of science rest on cause and effect, so what was the first cause, and where did it come from? That is just one example of the fallacy of depending on science to explain creation.

Even Darwin, before the end of his life, noted that, in his travels, he should have found hundreds of missing links, yet had found none. The main problem with evolution is it depends on positive mutation. To the best of my knowledge, science has never found even one positive mutation or bridge from one animal to another, and you would need millions of them to progress from a single cell to a human being.

In effect, you choose to believe science, which on the origin of the universe, proves itself wrong every few decades and needs to adjust its thinking, or you choose to believe the Bible, which has never been proven wrong in any subject it touches. If you were on a jury listening to evidence, who would you believe: a witness who has proven to be habitually mistaken or a witness who has never been proven wrong?

There are more demographics in this group, but I have covered the highlights.

Are you in group two and embraced Jesus in a rocky place? Was life so disastrous that climbing over the rock pile became all-consuming and Jesus got lost in the shuffle? Perhaps your situation was that your family was so anti-Christian you were unable to overcome the opposition and let Jesus slip into the background. Or perhaps it was the place you lived and the people you hung out with. When they refused to

What Are We Trying To Accomplish?

accept your decision, you were not in a position to stand up for Jesus. It is not uncommon for a person's situation to discourage them from living for Jesus. I understand it because I have lived it.

I have heard many preachers and evangelists state without reservation that if you cannot point to the time when you invited Jesus into your heart, you are not saved. I will take every one of them to task, because I grew up in a very toxic Christian home, but Christian enough to have communicated to me the concept of salvation. To this day, I cannot point to a specific time when my knowledge of Jesus moved from intellectual to saving faith. However, I can guarantee beyond a shadow of a doubt that it did happen.

Because of the toxic environment, I grew up a confused and unhappy teenager. Like many in a similar environment, I turned to alcohol and a rough crowd. I gravitated to that crowd because they did not care who you were or what you did as long as you did not bother them. They were comfortable to be around because they did not ask anything of you and did not expect you to ask anything of them. They did not condemn you for how you lived and did nothing to change you. In other words, they did nothing to add more rocks to the pile. During these hard years, in the back of my head was always the knowledge that if something happened to me, I would wind up in heaven because my reliance was on Jesus. As a result, my personal experience tells me it is absolutely possible for a saved person to go completely off the rails because of the rock pile.

Recently a movie called *Unbroken* ran in the theaters. It is the story of Louis Zamperini, a troubled youth who eventually turned to sports. He became a distance runner in high school and qualified for the 1936 Olympic team in the five-thousand-meter race. During World War II, he was a bombardier in a B-24 Liberator, and mechanical difficulties caused his plane to crash into the ocean. Louis and two others escaped alive and were stranded on a life raft. One of the other men died and was given a burial at sea, while Louis and the other man survived on the raft for the next forty-six days. At one point during this time, Louis reverted to his Catholic background and prayed that if God would let him live,

GOD'S *Love* LANGUAGE

he would dedicate the rest of his life to Him. The men were eventually rescued by the Japanese and sent to a POW camp.

The commander of the POW camp was a particularly sadistic person nicknamed the Bird. The Bird took special delight in trying to break Louis when he discovered that he was an Olympian. He dreamed up everything he could to torture Louis in every way possible, but Louis hung tough through it all. After the war, Louis returned home, but the agony of his time in the POW camp haunted him for years. He kept up appearances as he went on numerous speaking tours as a genuine war hero, but underneath he was a mess.

He suffered constant nightmares about his time in the POW camp and turned to alcohol and partying to numb the pain. His life was unraveling, and he began lashing out at his wife and children. The rock pile in his world kept getting bigger and bigger, and he could not climb over it. He dreamt of returning to Japan to find the Bird and kill him. He believed this was the only way he could ever rid himself of the torturous nightmares. His rock pile had become so large he was unable to even think about the promise he had made to God at sea.

In 1949, Louis met Jesus face-to-face at a Billy Graham crusade and, like the apostle Paul, his life was changed forever. The nightmares vanished, and the thoughts of revenge disappeared. He finally fulfilled his promise and surrendered the rest of his life to Christ. He quit his business and started a camp for troubled youth, hoping to help them avoid some of the mistakes he had made.

During a speaking tour in Japan, Louis had the opportunity to meet most of the guards who had been in his POW camp. Upon seeing the guards coming his way, he ran to meet them and threw his arms around them. They immediately withdrew from him, unable to comprehend this expression of forgiveness. When Louis explained where his forgiveness came from, all but one of the guards came to Christ. Louis wanted desperately to meet with Sergeant Watanabe, the Bird, but the sergeant refused to see him. Louis then wrote a letter to the sergeant explaining how he felt and sent it to him.

What Are We Trying To Accomplish?

The point of the story as it relates to this book is that it does not matter how high your rock pile is because Jesus is bigger. If you are being crushed spiritually by the rocks, He can rescue you. He can flatten that rock pile to a smooth and level road.

Many different kinds of rock piles can throw us off course. Family tragedy is a very common one. Why did my father, mother, brother, sister, aunt, uncle, cousin, or whoever get cancer, have that car accident and become disabled, or die in a natural disaster? Why did I lose my job, or why did my business fail so I could not pay my bills? Another rock pile—you can fill in the blank with many possible scenarios. In fact, an entire book could be written about the tragedies that befall us and create rock piles.

Group three is where I believe most Christians reside. They probably go to church on a regular basis, drop something in the collection plate if the monthly bills permit, and volunteer for a special event if nothing else is on the calendar. However, for the most part, they are so caught up in day-to-day life that Jesus is pretty far down on their to-do list. Statistically, if you are reading this book, you are most likely in this group.

You may be working hard at a job trying to stay afloat financially. You are raising your kids to the best of your ability, worrying about the world they are growing up in. Depending on the age of your kids, your concerns include the people they are hanging around with and how that can influence their thinking. You are concerned with society at large and how violent the world has become. If your children are out on a weekend night, you probably don't get much sleep until they get home.

I was born a few years before the baby boomers and grew up in the Cold War era. We used to have "drop drills," where the teacher, during a random school day, would turn around and yell, "Drop!" We would all crawl under our desks and curl up with our hands over our heads to protect us in case the Russians dropped "the bomb" – as if that was going to help! My fifteen-year-old granddaughter talks about "shooter drills," where they practice what to do if someone in the school has a gun. They secure the room so no one can get in, cover the windows so no one can see in, and take other such actions in an attempt to secure the space and protect their lives.

The high school I attended was one of the worst in the area because it was an expansion school. When an expansion school opens, the people in charge go to all the schools around and ask them to send students to fill the new school. Well, they don't send the good ones. Even in that environment, we never worried about someone entering our school and shooting everyone. The thought never entered our minds. My granddaughter, on the other hand, attends one of the finest high schools in Southern California, yet takes part in drills to protect the students from someone with a gun. It is quite a world she is growing up in.

You may worry about a downturn in the economy and how that will affect your 401(k) or your stock account. Perhaps your job is not keeping pace with the ever more expensive cost of living, so you are looking for a better job, a second job, or a side business. You are constantly hoping your big break is just around the corner.

The point is so much is going on in our lives, it is admittedly difficult to find time for God. I completely understand. I spent almost my entire life running the rat race, leaving God in second or third place. Only lately have I begun to organize my priorities correctly. Now, I get up in the morning and almost always have my *God time*. Of course, there are occasions when I have an early appointment that does not allow me the time, but otherwise, I sit down with a cup of coffee for my Bible reading and prayer. Don't misunderstand me; I am not a saint by any stretch of the imagination. Many mornings I have so much on my to-do list, or a project I desperately want to finish, that I hurry through that time. But generally, I stop and ask God to help me use the time wisely. Habits take a long time to properly establish. Here I am at seventy-five writing a book, but at least I beat Moses, who did not return to Egypt to lead the Jews to the Promised Land until he was eighty. It also took him forty years to get them to the Promised Land, but I am hoping this book does not take anywhere near that long to complete!

What Are We Trying To Accomplish?

The reality is we live in a busy and sometimes scary world. The weeds around us are trying to choke the life out of us, and it can be very hard to find the time or energy to consistently have our God time.

The fourth group consists of those believers who have gained control of their lives and set proper priorities. They are in the good soil, the soil of God's Word. They are receiving nutrients and the water of life from the Holy Spirit, and they are enjoying a life in God's service. These are not, for the most part, pastors or missionaries. They are everyday people who have somehow, through God's grace, managed to get it all together. These good-soil people are not very different from you and me, but they are often the ones who do the hidden tasks that allow *group three* to have a church to go to.

They give up doing things they might want to do in order to support the ministry. They are the ones who vacuum and dust the church and clean the bathrooms so that they are presentable for Sunday morning. They might forgo their plans to help a neighbor run an errand, in the name of Jesus. They do thousands of things the average person does not even think of, because they have the mind and spirit of Christ. They do it simply because it is the right thing to do. These people have figured out that whatever they have is not really theirs, but it is God's to use as He pleases.

If you read the first few chapters of Acts, you will find that the early church developed this mind-set. Those with wealth shared with those who lacked wealth and everyone worked together to build up the New Testament church out of its infancy. They all used their time, talents, and possessions – whatever they might have – in a communal effort to build the church. Through the selfless acts of these early church members, in one generation, the church spread throughout Europe and Asia. That is quite an accomplishment, but a people united in a common godly effort and willing to do whatever is necessary can accomplish some phenomenal things.

The title of this chapter asks, what are we trying to accomplish? If you look carefully at the first three groups discussed, in one way or another, they are all trying to get through this life in the best way possible. The issue becomes motivation. If you are a driven, ambitious person, your idea of the best way possible centers around the amount of wealth you can accumulate before you die. If you are family-driven, your best way possible is determined by whatever makes life better for your family. If you are single and looking for a mate, your best way possible to accomplish that goal is to focus on anything you can do to make yourself more attractive to the opposite sex. There are thousands of motivations, but the common denominator is self-interest, trying to make yourself happy through self-effort. An easy way to determine your motivation is by taking an honest appraisal to identify what you are working hardest to accomplish.

The people in the fourth group, on the other hand, are motivated by making God happy. Their sense of happiness is determined by accomplishing something for God. They are less concerned about their standard of living and more concerned about serving God. For the most part, they are the happiest and most contented of the four groups.

Paul, in Philippians 4:10–13, speaks about being content in any situation, whether well fed or hungry, living in plenty or want. Paul considered this life as a tool to accomplish something eternal. Whatever situation he found himself in was only a tool to accomplish an eternal result. If you have no earthly ambition for health, wealth, comfort, possessions, status, recognition, or any other thing the world has to offer, what can anyone take away from you that will affect your happiness? Anything you have is not for you – it is for God. I have to admit I am not there. I have a long way to go, but I am striving to get there.

Here is the good news of this chapter: you are not an immobile object like a seed stuck wherever it lands. *You can move from wherever you are to wherever you need to be anytime you are ready! And God is right there to help you move any time you ask.*

Chapter 3
WHAT DO WE EXPECT?

In my case, the expectations were that my business would succeed because I was attempting to do something that God clearly commands in His Word. I started the business in part because I expected to generate substantial sums of disposable income that could be used to help the less fortunate. I have read through the Bible enough times to know that taking care of widows, orphans, the poor, and the disabled is a very common theme. Therefore, according to my human logic, since God commands us to do this, my business had to succeed.

I have already addressed the fallacy of attempting to impose human logic on God's plan. I have no idea what positive things may come from the writing of this book, but I do know that if not for the experience of my failing business, this book would never have been written. So did God say, "Yes, I want you to go into this business to help people, but not quite in the way you expect"? I do not know; I am only starting to scratch the surface of understanding a little of the mind of God.

When you read the New Testament, you clearly see the apostles' expectation that Jesus would somehow throw off the shackles of the Roman government and restore Israel to a position of prominence on the world scene. Thus, when He died, they were crushed. They did not know what to do. Confusion reigned supreme; what were these three years of ministry about if not to restore the physical kingdom? Should they go back and try to pick up the pieces of their old lives? In their minds, the plans they had imagined as they followed Jesus died with Him on the cross. But then three days later, He came out of the tomb, and the whole picture changed. The world took on a whole new meaning when they realized their ideas of the restoration of the earthly kingdom were completely wrong. The dawn on that third morning arose on a new heavenly kingdom, one available to the entire world.

If you read the Gospels, you will notice that Jesus spoke continually about the kingdom of heaven, but apparently, the disciples were not listening. Finally, at His trial, Jesus clearly stated to Pilate, "My kingdom is not of this world." In spite of all this, the disciples did not grasp it, and when Jesus died, they did not know what to do because this was not the destination they had expected. Their response was, "What happened?"

The problem with expectations is we do not have the mind of God. God takes us down a certain road, and we begin to interpret the signs in our own way. When we realize the destination we expected is not where we are going, we get mad, and God becomes the bad guy. Or maybe we get the idea in our mind that God wants us to do "this," whatever "this" is. If the idea fails, we question God. We remind Him of the benefits that would have been available and what it could have accomplished, and once again, God is the bad guy.

Expectations have derailed many faithful Christians. We plan our lives, but then tragedy strikes in an unexpected way, such as the death of a spouse or a child. Our reaction is, "I have been trying to serve You, God, and You do this to me?" Or possibly some other tragedy befalls you. I do not know your worst nightmare, but if it happens, Satan will not lose a second before exploiting the opportunity to try to derail you in a time of tragedy. He lives for these opportunities and won't waste one of them.

But what is the reality? The reality is God has a plan, but we can miss seeing that because *our* plan crashed, and now we are mad at God. Think of someone like Joni Eareckson Tada. Would her worldwide ministry exist if she had not become a quadriplegic? But after her accident, she apparently went through a rough time, fully expecting God to heal

What Do We Expect?

her. When it didn't happen, she was in agony because God's plan did not match her plan.

In Psalm 44, the psalmist reflects on the stories of how God drove out the nations when Israel entered the Promised Land. He recounts how Israel flourished and drove out all the other nations, and how God helped them trample all their enemies. God is their boast all day long, and they will praise Him forever. But then, in verse 9, a change occurs.

The psalmist laments that God has rejected and humbled them, that He is no longer going out with their armies, that they are being scattered like sheep. In verse 17, the psalmist says this came upon them even though they had *not* forgotten God and had *not* been false to His covenant. Their hearts had *not* turned back; they had *not* strayed from his path. In verse 23, the psalmist cries, *"Awake, Lord! Rouse yourself! Do not reject us forever."* The psalmist seems to be saying, "We are doing everything right, but it is all going wrong. This is not what I expected!"

We have already looked at the first 17 verses of Psalm 73. To recap, the psalmist is questioning obedience. He is lamenting the fact that evil people are flourishing. This is much the same as Psalm 44. Both are saying that good things are happening to bad people. The wicked people are shaking their fists in God's face and daring Him to do something about it. The psalmist laments that he had tried his best to do what he was supposed to, but he was being afflicted and punished. No matter how he tried to rationalize this, it did not make sense.

Does any of this sound familiar? Have you ever wondered what God is doing, because it just isn't fair? Have you looked at your job or the business world and wondered why the cheaters get ahead? We will go into this in-depth later on.

Many of us have had hopes dashed. We have started something that we really felt led to do, and yet it all fell apart. I genuinely felt led to start my business, and when it kept losing money, I cried to the Lord in agony. I could not believe He was doing this to me. It hurt – not just a little hurt, but that deep ache in your chest that feels like you can't breathe.

GOD'S *Love* LANGUAGE

The Bible tells us that God is our Father, and depending on the dynamic in our family of origin, that will have a definite effect on our view of God. Generally speaking, we will view God in a similar way to how we view our earthly father. This is not always the case, but if your father was a kind, loving, and understanding father, you will probably view God in the same way. If your father was a strict disciplinarian, your view of God will probably be that He is waiting for you to do something wrong so He can punish you. If your father was not around for whatever reason, you may have trouble connecting with God. While this is generally true, the opposite can also happen: you want a loving father so much that once you find God, you cling to Him as you were not able to cling to your earthly father. The point is our life experiences flavor our view of God, and those experiences also flavor our expectations.

Christianity has a hard time surviving properly in the minds of those in an affluent society. Law enforcement studies show the crime rate is lower in places where everyone is in a similar financial position. If everyone is in the same financial position, whether that position is poor or affluent, the expectations of what people think they deserve decreases. They are as well off as everyone else, so they are not as inclined to want more.

Likewise, if all our friends and acquaintances are in a similar life situation as we are, the expectation of a better or easier life also goes way down. After all, aren't we all God's children? But that is not the case. I do not care which church you belong to or which Christian circle you run in; there will always be those who seem to breeze through life. Most of the people in your group will experience the normal run of the mill problems, spousal disagreements, raising kids, finances and all the others. Then there are the ones who always seem to struggle in one way or another. Tragedy seems to follow them around like their shadow. If you are in group three and know some group one people it can be a trying experience to make sense of it. Depending on which group you are in and your spiritual condition it will reflect in your expectations.

What Do We Expect?

As we raise our kids, we generally encourage them to raise their expectations, telling them not to settle for "whatever." With a little more effort or a little more study, we say, they can get into a better university and ultimately obtain a better job and have more. Or some other similar scenario may be in play.

We also live in a society that constantly tells us we need more. Turn on the TV, and 30 percent of what you see is someone telling you about something you can't live without. Society is constantly bombarding us with the thought that we should expect more.

Our expectation for the blessings seems to generally run toward physical or monetary blessings. Someone testifies that they quit their job because they found out the business was doing something unethical, and the very next week, they got a new and better job, implying the Lord "blessed" them for their godly ethical behavior and for quitting their job by faith. These are the stories that grab us, and every time we hear stories like these, we feel encouraged to act in a similar way. But what happens when we step out in faith, and it all falls apart? This is not in our expectation résumé. This is not supposed to happen.

In my experience, when someone is speaking about blessings, they are usually speaking about receiving something this world has to offer: "God blessed me with a new house," or "God blessed me with a new car," "God blessed me with a raise at work," or whatever else you can imagine. I can only wonder how many people pray each week that God will help them win the lottery.

An honest evaluation of people, in general, will show that with rare exception, we all – and I include myself – are looking for something this world has to offer, and the more I think about it, the more I have to wonder why. Revelation 21 begins with John talking about a new heaven and earth because the first heaven and earth had passed away. This earth and everything in it will someday cease to exist, yet we worry about what we have and what we don't have. James, in chapter 4, vs. 1-3 of his letter states:

> What causes fights and quarrels among you? Don't they come from your desires that battle within you? You want something but don't get it. You kill and covet but you cannot have what you want. You quarrel and fight. You do not have, because you do not ask God. When you ask you do not receive because you ask with wrong motives, that you may spend what you get on your pleasures.

A careful study of James reveals that James is saying in human terms what Paul elucidates in heavenly terms. In the Saturday morning men's bible study I attend, we just went through the book of James. Once I realized that James is only expressing a different viewpoint, not a different idea, the book began making more sense. The wording in the above passage, you kill and covet because you don't get what you want. As I pondered that verbiage, it occurred to me that the first murder in the bible was because Cain did not get what he wanted. In almost every situation, our expectation is that if we are good Christians, do what is right, and attempt to honor God, He will bless us. And our idea of blessing is generally some tangible thing. Eventually, we will take a serious look at that premise in an attempt to determine what God's blessing is really all about.

Chapter 4

WHAT HAPPENS WHEN WE DO NOT GET WHAT WE EXPECT?

The answer to that question depends entirely on our spiritual condition. I believe I would be safe in saying that for most Christians, the first reaction is disappointment. The level of disappointment generally has a wide range, anywhere from a momentary thought to a knockdown drag-out fight with God. Our thoughts may go like this: *God, I have been praying for this for a long time. I have had friends join me in prayer about this. I filled out a prayer card at church. I really felt this was a good thing. God, I could have used this to help the church, other people, missionaries* [or any other good thing that may come to your mind]. *God, this would have been a good thing, and now it is gone forever.* Our disappointment can hang around in the back of our minds for days, weeks, or even much longer. Depending on the gravity of the unanswered prayer, it can deeply affect our lives, our relationships with other people, and our relationship with God.

In 2 Timothy 4, Paul asks Timothy to do his best to come to him quickly. Demas, because of his love of the world, had deserted Paul and gone to Thessalonica. Did Demas desert Paul because his expectations were not met? Did Demas think a missionary trip with Paul would be a "glamorous" experience? When they arrived at their destination, did Demas find the living quarters were not as luxurious as he expected? Did the experience prove to be a lot harder than he anticipated? Maybe he was expecting the people to fawn all over him because he was working with the apostle Paul, and when that did not happen, he grew discouraged. Whatever occurred, Demas probably had a mental picture of what a missionary journey with Paul would be like, and when it proved to be something else, he deserted.

Has that ever happened to you? You plan an outing with a mental picture of what the outing will be like, but when you get to the destination, it is not as big, as exciting, as interesting, or as _____ as you expected (you fill in the blank). Generally, when that happens, disappointment sets in, and you are not able to enjoy the outing for whatever it does have to offer. How different could the outing have been if you had gone without any preconceived notion and experienced it for what it had to offer?

One does not have to travel too far or talk to very many people to hear stories about someone leaving a church, a spouse, an extended family, or even God because their expectations were not met. Unfortunately, we form expectations in our minds about the way things should be, and when they are not met, we cut and run.

For instance, years ago, my mother had a problem with one of her brothers. I either never knew or have long since forgotten what she supposedly did or said that started the feud, but it dragged on for a long time. I stopped by his house one time to see if anything could be done to rectify the situation. One of the other brothers happened to be present and witnessed the verbal exchange. I asked the offended brother if there was anything my mother could do to fix the rift. His answer was no. I responded, "Well, you are a churchgoing man, and I know you read your Bible. God says if our brother [or sister] has offended us and comes to us to apologize, we are to forgive seventy times seven." His answer was, "I passed that number a long time ago." The other brother later told me he could not believe his brother's stubbornness. But that is how it can go with us. Our expectations are not met, and the results can be disastrous.

I do not know what the divorce rate is right now, but it is probably around 40 percent – and I may be underestimating that. The percentage

What Happens When We Do Not Get What We Expect?

does not matter as much as the reasons. Now admittedly, there are some absolutely legitimate divorces, such as an unfaithful spouse, abuse, or abandonment, but too often, it is something like "irreconcilable differences." Irreconcilable differences? In layman's terms, it means, "We are not on the same page, and neither of us is willing to negotiate to the middle."

There are not two totally compatible people in this world, and if any couple says differently, it is only because they have both learned to ignore the negatives and enjoy the positives. But for those who cannot figure out how to do that, it is easier just to quit and try again with someone else. The problem is the divorce rate for second marriages is even higher. I guess that doesn't work either.

Our expectations with God run the same obstacle course. We can read the Bible in one of two ways. We can look for what we want it to say and ignore the rest, or we can honestly attempt to ascertain what God is trying to tell us. Unfortunately, our human nature seems to run to the former. I know that when my business was failing, in my morning Bible reading, I found every verse that promised success. Depending on how you cherry-pick verses, you can make the Bible say almost anything. Over the years, countless cults have been based on selective reading of the Bible, and many still exist today. It is possible to start a "cult" in your own mind by selectively reading the Bible. I know, I did.

It has only been lately, as I've read through the Bible, that I have seen things like the following (all emphases added):

> For just as the *sufferings* of Christ flow over into our lives, so also through Christ our comfort overflows.
> —2 Corinthians 1:5

> For it has been granted to you on behalf of Christ not only to believe on him, but also to *suffer* for him.
> —Philippians 1:29

> Consider it pure *joy*, my brothers, whenever you face *trials* of many kinds.
> —James 1:2

> Jesus said, "In this world you *will* have *trouble*. But take heart, I have overcome the world."
> —John 16:33

If you really pay attention reading the Bible It is hard to find many places where it does not show in one way or another that God very often works through suffering. I do not know how many times I have read through the Bible but only recently am I focusing on that fact. It seems that my mind wanted to skip over the hard stuff and only concentrate on the good stuff.

If you read the Bible regarding the birth of John the Baptist, you will notice that John, like Jesus, was a miracle baby. For many years, his mother was unable to conceive, but six months prior to the Holy Spirit's planting Jesus in Mary's womb, John's mother became pregnant despite her advanced age. When Mary became pregnant, she went to visit Zechariah and Elizabeth, John's parents. They were relatives, and possibly Mary needed some motherly advice. But for whatever reason, she went. When Elizabeth saw Mary, John leapt within her womb. Even in his gestational state, John realized Jesus was the messiah.

John and Jesus were related, possibly first or second cousins. It is not unreasonable to assume they spent time together growing up. John became the last of the Old Testament prophets, baptizing and testifying about the coming Messiah, Jesus. John knew that he was the forerunner of the messiah. Yet when his ministry was completed, and he had fulfilled his divine purpose, John was thrown into prison. This prompted him to send a message to Jesus asking, "Are you the one who is to come, or are we looking for another?"

Now, why would John ask that question? He knew that his purpose was to teach and baptize, preparing the populace for the coming

What Happens When We Do Not Get What We Expect?

messiah. He knew Jesus was that messiah. He knew it when he was still in the womb. When some of his disciples left to follow Jesus and then other disciples questioned it, his reply was, "He must increase and I must decrease." With all that knowledge and history behind him, where *did* that question come from? For thirty years, he had heard the Messiah was coming to restore the kingdom of Israel. Did John believe, like so many others, that Jesus had come to set up the earthly kingdom? When his expectations were not met, and he saw no evidence of the Roman occupation diminishing, did his faith in Jesus waver?

One of my personal heroes in the Bible is Joseph of the Old Testament. He was sold into slavery by his own brothers and brought by caravan to Egypt. In Egypt, he was sold to Potiphar, a wealthy, powerful man. Because he honored God in every way, all that he touched prospered; but God had a divine purpose in mind for his prospering, so you can't use this to claim that God always wants to bless us financially. Potiphar, realizing there was something special about Joseph, put him in charge of everything. Potiphar's wife, however, took a sexual interest in Joseph, and when he spurned her advances, she made false accusations about him and had Potiphar throw Joseph into prison.

The man in charge of the prison also realized Joseph was special, so he too put Joseph in charge. Joseph languished in prison for years but ultimately became the second in command over all Egypt, the second-most powerful man on the planet at that time. Only Pharaoh was more powerful. Through all this, there is no mention of Joseph ever questioning God, complaining about his situation, or grumbling about the injustice of it all. No, he just made the best of every situation. I can only imagine that I would have kicked and screamed about my brothers and the woman who lied about me and put me into prison for something I did not do. I would have been screaming it from the rooftops. Unless you are a whole lot different from the vast majority of humanity, you would have done the same.

We were created in the image of God, and although that original creation was corrupted by sin, we still carry the tendencies of God. One of those tendencies is our sense of justice. God is a just God in everything He does, and we carry, to varying degrees, that same sense of justice in our minds.

Living in the Los Angeles area with its size and diversity there is always tragedy on the evening news. Someone gets caught in a gang shooting and is wounded or killed. A speeding driver hits someone in a crosswalk and that person is killed. Guns come out blazing over a road rage incident, or some other kind of tragedy. When the friends or relatives of the victim are interviewed on the evening news the conversation generally swings to, "I just want the person responsible to come forward so we can get some Justice for our relative or friend". Justice is part of our DNA, and when we feel we have been unjustly treated, we have a lot to say about it.

As Christians, we want to focus our justice on God when we feel He has wronged us. We get into the comparison game. We look at someone who has possibly gone through what we are facing and came out just fine, but in our case, things are falling apart. We compare the situations and complain to God about the injustice of it all: "It just isn't fair, God. Why am I suffering and they did not?" One thing I've noticed is, when someone is playing the comparison game, myself included, is that they never look at someone worse off than they are. I do not care what your situation is; someone somewhere has had it worse in one way or another. But interestingly, we never compare ourselves to them; that would defeat the whole purpose of the comparison game. Because our expectations were not met, we want to point to something that will strengthen our argument of injustice.

Another thing I have noticed in my life and in the lives of others is we have selective memory. When we are wronged, we remember it for a very long time, but when we wrong someone else, we lose that memory very quickly. Talk to any married couple individually and ask them, "What has your spouse done wrong that you never mentioned to them?" Ask them to be totally honest in their answers, and I guarantee both will remember things the other one does not remember at

What Happens When We Do Not Get What We Expect?

all. Likewise, when we feel God has wronged us, we tuck that into a compartment in our brain and generally keep the memory alive for a long time. But before we go to sleep at the end of the day, we cannot remember the things we've done. The reality is that we are the ones who should apologize to God instead of holding onto petty injustices.

The title of this chapter asked what happens when we don't get what *we* want. What about what God wants? What we want almost universally is something of this world. When we get into a bad place because of an unexpected happening, we should spend more time asking, "What does God want? What am I supposed to learn from this? What do I need to change as a result of what I have learned?" In other words, why don't we look at the situation through God's eyes?

Disappointment is the result of unrealized expectations. When an expectation is unrealized, we begin to wonder what is going to happen. So now, we begin to worry about the ramifications and start to plot and scheme about how we will correct the situation. We then fast-forward to tomorrow, next week, or even next year to extend our worry. God, however, cautions us about worry, and the reason He does is because when we worry, we are encroaching on His territory. We do not know the future. We do not know how the situation fits into His grand plan. Nonetheless, we are determined to fix it. But how are we going to fix something when we do not know why it is happening, how it fits in with everything else that God is doing, and what the final result needs to be? Only God has that information, so why do we try to control it?

A movie I once saw concerned a man who felt his life had taken a wrong turn when he struck out in a baseball game as a high schooler and caused his team to lose. As I recall the plot, he agonized over that strikeout constantly. Then, through a series of events, he was able to relive that moment, but instead, he hit a home run and won the game. Instantly and without him realizing it, his whole life changed. Initially, he thought it was for the better, but eventually, he discovered the change was for the worse. He then spent the rest of the movie trying to get back to his former life. In retrospect, that strikeout, though painful at the time, was necessary to put him on the path where he belonged.

The point is we do not know the plot of our vignette or what it is designed to accomplish. It is entirely possible we will not ever know on this side of eternity. You have no way of knowing who is paying attention to the story. Imagine you were the one who struck out. The way you respond to that same strikeout may affect someone watching you and alter their life forever. Your positive response may help some person make the correct decision about the fork in the road they are facing, while a negative response may prompt the opposite reaction. In the movie, many lives were affected in countless ways when the man's life changed from what it was to his new life. He was married to a different person, had a different job, and on and on. But in the end, it was all wrong.

When we decide to do everything God's way, the result is always positive. Our situation may be very painful or scary or both, but when God puts it together with all the other things He has been doing, the result will always be positive. We may not know in this life what good came of it, but we must believe God when He assures us that He works all things together for good. The problem is we always try to look for the good that will come *our* way for what we went through, when in reality, the good may be for someone else who does something great that would have never happened otherwise.

Faith and worry are opposite sides of the same coin. True faith believes that whatever we are going through is part of God's plan and will turn out for God's intended purpose. Worry occurs when we are looking for our own good and not recognizing that God is always in control, and that our comfort is not necessarily the end result.

I can declare from experience that every time something goes wrong in my life, my first thought is about myself and how this is affecting me. Only recently have I been able to move beyond my selfish first thoughts and wonder what God is going to do. To be perfectly honest, I have not seen any positive things happening yet in my particular case, but I have

What Happens When We Do Not Get What We Expect?

actually stopped worrying about it. I still have a roof over my head, food in the pantry, and I am keeping up with the bills. Beyond that, everything else belongs to God. If it isn't part of today, it is His to worry about, and much of what is part of today is still His to worry about.

I am attempting to take God along with me in everything I am doing. It is a new concept for me because I have been very self-reliant all my life. Oftentimes my self-reliance borders on arrogance, and I suppose, in many instances, it does in fact, cross the line. For me to attempt to completely change and bring God along in what I feel quite confident in doing myself is challenging, to say the least. But let me tell you what is happening as a result.

I am presently trying to put together an old Pontiac. My workspace is very limited, so my garage and side yard both look like an explosion happened in an auto salvage yard. Before my attempt to bring God along, I spent half my time looking for things, even items that I was just holding in my hand and had laid down someplace. I would walk around and ask God to help me find things... to no avail. It finally dawned on me that I was telling God to sit in the corner of the garage and only show up when there was something I could not do for myself. That was not asking God to be a part of my life; that was asking God to be a part-time helper.

Lately, in my morning God time, I have begun asking God to be with me, helping everything in my day to go well. To my surprise, I find my days are going much more smoothly. As I work, I try to talk to God constantly, but occasionally I fall back into my "I can do it" mode. I start misplacing things and once again waste time looking for an item I was just holding in my hand. When I do that, I stop and apologize to God for leaving Him behind, and I ask Him to come along with me. In almost every instance, whatever I have been looking for appears. I never neglect to say "Thank you" out loud.

The point is our expectations almost always run to what will benefit us, while God looks at the whole picture and what will benefit His overall plan. He desperately wants us to be a part of the plan and to play an important role in it, but that will never happen until we are willing to say to Him continually, "Will you come along with me and take Your place in my life?" When we truly have that attitude, it does not matter what happens. We will recognize that whatever is happening, no matter how it affects us personally, has an important place in God's overall plan.

I believe what makes it difficult is we often are looking to do some big thing that will bring us recognition. The reason is we are basically a selfish lot. Even when we do something unselfish, we hope to garner some kind of recognition. When we are born, we are totally self-absorbed. We enter the world screaming *I want!* A baby does not care if Mom is having a really bad day, is utterly exhausted, has a cold or the flu, or is dealing with something that is sabotaging her day. The baby just wants: *I want my bottle, my diaper changed, to be held, to be rocked,* or any other thing that may enter that young mind. The totality of that baby's thought pattern is *I want*.

If we are really honest with ourselves, are we any different with God? How much of our prayer life is, "Father, help me with this problem, "Take this issue away," or "Help me find the money to pay the bills"? Or maybe it's, "I can't take this problem anymore," or "I have been dealing with this issue for months now, so why can't it be over?" Even Jesus fell prey to this syndrome.

In the Garden of Gethsemane, just before His arrest, what did He pray? He agonized over His coming crucifixion to the point that he was sweating drops of blood, and He prayed, "Father, if possible, can this cup pass from Me?" In His humanity, He agonized over what He was about to face and asked if there was some way to avoid it. Jesus, who knew from the origin of the universe that it was going to be necessary for Him to die to save humanity from their sin, in a totally human moment asked if there was another way. But He did not stop there. We have no way of knowing how much time passed before He resolved the situation, but at the end, He prayed:

What Happens When We Do Not Get What We Expect?

"Not My will but Thine be done."

The sin is not in being human; the sin is in dwelling in our humanity for extended lengths of time before we finally let go and give it to God. When we finally give it to God and don't take it back, as we are so prone to do, He promises to help us and give us peace that the situation will work out for the best, and He takes away our anxiety. It all depends on faith, our faith to believe God.

If you read the Old Testament, time and again, you will find the Israelites were instructed to look back to the destruction of Egypt and their miraculous escape from slavery. It was their anchor. It was a visual picture of God's deliverance in one of the most desperate times in their history. It was a reminder of God's power, and more than that, a reminder of God's love and concern for His people. We have a similar visual picture that Scripture constantly admonishes us to reflect on because it is the ultimate expression of God's love – the crucifixion, death, burial, and resurrection of Jesus. I do not believe we have a true mental picture of what that fully expresses.

Go back a couple of paragraphs to where Jesus prayed to have the cup removed. There was the obvious physical pain, but beyond that, there was the mental pain. Almost all of us, at one time or another, have done something so bad that the mental agony haunted us for a very long time afterward. Imagine having not only the guilt of your transgression hanging over you, but also the guilt of every person who had ever or would ever live. Now imagine putting yourself on the cross in that tremendous physical and mental pain and looking up to your Father for help. But He has turned His back on you because He could not stand to look at all that sin. Jesus and the Father had been together for eternity. I am not speaking figuratively, but literally, and now they were separated by our sins. No wonder Jesus cried out in agony, "My God, My God, why have *you* forsaken Me?"

We should reflect on that constantly when we are in distress, remembering what Paul declared in Romans 8:31–32: *"What shall we then say in response to this? If God is for us, who can be against us? He who spared not his own son but gave him up for us all—how will he not also, along with him, graciously give us all things."*

When James urges us to consider our trials pure joy, I do not believe he is speaking of anything of great noteworthiness, but simply the generalities of daily life. For example, you are in a hurry to make an appointment, and the traffic is stopped for some reason. Instead of automatically assuming that God is not helping you, why not ask God to help you to calm down and adjust to the situation? As you do this and see God working in small situations, you will build up memories that will enable you to trust Him for the big things.

Several years ago, my doctor was about seven months pregnant with her first child. She was on her way somewhere when another driver cut her off at a toll booth. At the very next intersection, that car was T-boned by a driver who ran a red light. If that other driver had not cut her off, she is the one who would have been hit. An incident that, in today's climate, could have resulted in road rage actually saved her from an accident that could have easily caused considerable damage to her or her unborn child.

We need to exercise caution before making a judgment about any situation because we have no way of knowing what might have happened if the situation had *not* upset our schedule. We will always have both good days and bad days. Generally speaking, if we are honest with ourselves, we will admit we learn very little from the good days. It is the days that require us to work and sweat to get ourselves through a totally unexpected problem that supply the learning experiences.

It is the same with our spiritual growth. The good days with God, as pleasant as they are, are not the learning days. When the hard days come, we need to consider the trials as pure joy because God is actually taking the time to train us for something. He is trusting us to hang in there and learn. Of all the methods God could have used to accomplish His purpose, He chose us in all our reluctance and inability.

The wonder is God trusts *us* to accomplish something for *Him* if we are willing to learn.

Chapter 5

HAVE YOU EVER BEEN SPIRITUALLY STRANDED IN THE DESERT?

Oftentimes, in our Christian lives, we find ourselves in a spiritual holding pattern, flying around the airport as we wait for a runway to land on. We are flying in circles, going nowhere, but we know we can't land just anywhere. We are at the mercy of the controller at the airport, the weather, the congestion of other aircraft, and who knows what else. The point is we are stuck in the airplane, and we have absolutely no control over our circumstances.

As you read this chapter, I want you to keep two things in mind: (1) God loves you. This is the part of the message we like to hear, but the rest of the story is that God loves you too much to leave you where you are. That is the part we don't like to hear. (2) If God is not moving you, He is teaching you.

Oftentimes, this helpless condition occurs as a result of our belief that to be of worth, we need to be doing something. This frequently happens in my life because of my early childhood. I cannot point to any time in my life when either of my parents hugged me and told me they loved me. They grew up in equally loveless homes, so they did not know how to share love. Looking for meaning, I discovered that working elicited recognition, so I did my best to find something productive to do.

I worked in my parents' business for the better part of twenty years, and our relationship was so strange that many long-time customers did

GOD'S *Love* LANGUAGE

not know they were my parents or that I was their son. In order to maintain my sanity, I became an employee when at work and a son when the doors were locked. At work, my parents were the boss man and boss woman. After work, they could be Dad and Mom. At work, I could gain recognition for being a really good employee, willing to do anything to the best of my ability, but after work, I was just Dwight, not worthy of any real recognition. I was stuck in a situation over which I had little or no control. To numb things, I turned to alcohol. It did nothing to help the situation, but at least I could forget it for a while.

When my dad decided to retire, he desperately wanted me to buy the business, but I did not want it. It was an auto-repair business, and for years I watched my dad leave work looking emotionally like an unarmed man in a hatchet fight. I am not a people person, and I could not imagine dealing with the general public on a daily basis and putting up with what my dad did. In retrospect, I believe my parents wanted me to have the business because it was the only way they could show me love, and I denied them that.

When my parents finally sold the business, I realized we had little in common. Even though we lived only a few miles apart, I seldom saw them. If they needed help, I was right there to do whatever I could. I have always had a knack for fixing almost anything. While my father was much better at a lot of things, I always had a much broader base of knowledge and could fix many things that he would not even attempt to fix. But if there was nothing to fix, I was useless and stayed away. Admittedly, I was a lousy son, but I did not know how to be a son.

As a matter of fact, I have been a loner for my entire life because I do not know what to do with people. As a result, my spiritual feelings often run to, *what is my job, God? If I do not have a job, what good am I to You?* For long stretches, God did not allow me to do much, leaving me feeling like I was lost in the desert, looking for a road sign.

If you are like me, your thoughts sometimes run to, *what have I done, God, to make You mad?* or, *what have I not done that I should have done to make You happy?* In one way or another, some of us assume

Have You Ever Been Spiritually Stranded In The Desert?

responsibility for the disconnect between God and us. In my case, it was and, in some cases, still is because of the disconnect between my parents and myself. For others, this can be a natural assumption because of their relationships with other people. If our spouse is down for some reason, it is not uncommon for us to ask whether we have done something wrong. If a friend seems to be giving us the cold shoulder, we may ask the same question. Because we are imperfect people, most of us have learned we can innocently do the wrong thing and offend someone else.

The truth is many things can land us in the desert. I have seen more than one Christian who has been very involved in the church or some ministry and they eventually feel as though they have stagnated. They might try to change the way they approach their ministry in an attempt to pump new life into it. They might try prayer, their own or as a request of others. Sometimes they will hit the reset button, hoping that will somehow magically defrag the system and fix the problem.

Unfortunately, it may just be that the ministry has run its course and is no longer needed, or possibly their involvement is no longer required. God will sometimes take a person out of a ministry because they have experienced all the growth they can there and need to move on. If that happens and they do not have the faith to move on, they might wind up in the desert. It oftentimes stems from a feeling of being abandoned by God.

Any life-changing event has the potential of putting us in the desert. One very common event is the death of someone important to us. A parent, a friend, a mentor, or someone who has had a dramatic effect on us is now gone. We can no longer go to that person for help or advice. They may have helped us through many uncertain times or helped us gain clarity at a fork in the road. They had walked through many difficult experiences of their own and offered us invaluable advice, and now we are lost in the desert, looking for the road sign.

Another common experience that shakes us is the loss of a job. It could be a job we loved or one that defined us, but because of a merger, a relocation, or possibly retirement, it is now gone. Whatever the reason for its loss, we no longer have a definition of who or what we are, and consequently, we wander in the desert.

Other times, we find ourselves living a normal life, but it seems to have lost its purpose. Quite often, those around us have no idea we are in a very uncomfortable place. The desert can be a mental condition that does not prevent us from living a normal life; we can still enjoy our family, take the wife out for dinner, play games with the kids, or go on a picnic or to the movies. We can keep up with our jobs and all of our responsibilities, but through it all, we sense something is not right, that life has lost its purpose, or that I have lost all sense of control.

One of the interesting things about the desert is that two people with similar lifestyles experiencing similar troublesome situations may have completely different reactions. One might gravitate closer to God, looking for comfort and possibly answers, while the other is driven into the desert. Why would that be? There are many reasons for our reactions, and for the most part, they are a reflection of our background. We all have things to which we are sensitive. I know what mine are, and if you have ever reflected on your motivations, you know what yours are.

The other reason for our differing responses arises from the fact that trouble comes from two sources. The first and most familiar is the devil and all his minions; they are constantly working to derail any Christian in any way they can. Depending on who and where you are, the powers of darkness will throw something in your path to derail you. Think of all the famous preachers and Bible teachers who have been derailed and sent to the sidelines by an affair. Yes, it is alarming, but we do not know how long the devil hammered them and how many women it took to cause the fall; or what might have been going on in their life that put them in a weakened condition making them more vulnerable

The reality is that every one of us has weaknesses in our character that we fight on a regular basis. I am not a football fan, but I do know something about the game. The team with the ball will not call a play that attacks the defense at its strongest point, but will try in every way to exploit the known weaknesses. Similarly, it is the general M.O. of

Have You Ever Been Spiritually Stranded In The Desert?

the Devil. He won't attack you where you are strongest, but where you are weakest.

The other source of testing comes from God. That may be a shocker, but God uses trouble in your life to assist your growth. He uses it to mold your character. Hebrews 12:6 says that whom the Lord *loves* He disciplines. As a general rule, God will attack us at our strong point. He does that to show us we need Him even when we feel strong enough to get by without Him in a particular situation. So, the problem the two people of similar lifestyles with different reactions are facing may well have come from two different sources. Satan sent one to derail, and God sent one to teach—yes, identical problems, but one from God and one from Satan. The one from God was to teach, and the one from Satan was sent to disrupt. The difference lies in the people and their strong and weak points.

To use an example that everyone can relate to, chocolate. I have met people who do not like chocolate – not something I can understand. I happen to have a sweet tooth that runs clear to the bone, and if chocolate is around, I cannot leave it alone. A flippant example, perhaps but it is just meant to underscore that people react to stimuli differently. Another interesting thought to keep in mind is that the same situation at different times in your life can come from either source.

The desert is not necessarily a bad place. At the beginning of Jesus' ministry, after His baptism and the Holy Spirit's descent on Him, He was driven into the desert, where He spent forty days. I would speculate He was there to get alone with His Father because He was about to begin His formal ministry. He knew He had only three years before He would become the ultimate sacrifice for sin. Up until the Holy Spirit descended on Him at his baptism, Jesus was as human as any other person walking on the planet. The indwelling of the Holy Spirit was, at that time, not the norm. Even though Jesus' life is recorded in the New Testament, He was living in Old Testament times. While there were definitely people in the Old Testament times that had the benefit of the indwelling Holy Spirit, they were few and were in some way, noteworthy to the time.

The average person did not have that advantage. Apparently, up until the time of his baptism by John, Jesus did not have it either. The Bible clearly states that *after* His baptism, the Holy Spirit descended on him like a dove.

That may sound strange because if you read the first chapter of Hebrews, you clearly understand that Jesus was the creator, the one who made all things. I believe that includes the plan of redemption, if I am correct, when Jesus created everything, He also set Himself up for the cross. That, however, was in His divine state. When He went into the desert, He was in his human state, subject to all the pain and fears we all have. I can only speculate, but when the Holy Spirit came upon Him to commence His formal ministry, perhaps it became apparent to Jesus in a way that it had not before. Then He knew how difficult His ministry and how painful His sacrifice would be, both physically and emotionally.

If so, did Jesus need those forty days in the desert to communicate with His Father in a way that only the desert experience could provide? Or possibly did Jesus not know His end in that immersed human state? Were special instructions necessary to prepare Jesus for the difficult three years to follow and the horrific end of those years? In Hebrews 5:7–8, the author states, *"During the days of Jesus' life on earth, he offered up prayers and petitions with loud cries and tears to the one who could save him from death, and he was heard because of his reverent submission. Although he was a son, he learned obedience from what he suffered."* That passage seems to indicate that Jesus, at some point in His humanity, knew the kind of death He was facing. It must have been a very difficult burden to carry. Admittedly, this contains some speculation, but I believe it deserves consideration. In any case, it is without speculation that we know Jesus spent forty days and nights in the desert before starting his formal ministry. If he needed that time for preparation, don't we?

Consider the widow in Luke 21:2, who put two small coins into the collection plate. Jesus, commenting on this, remarked that she had

Have You Ever Been Spiritually Stranded In The Desert?

put in more than all the others. Everyone else gave out of their wealth, but she gave all she had. Jesus used this poor widow to teach about faith.

The widow expressed tremendous faith in giving up everything in her possession. She was now destitute, without any money at all. What was she going to eat, and where would she stay? She gave up all she had and now had to trust God to supply. Now let's think about the backstory.

This woman must have been a destitute widow for quite a period of time in order for Jesus' observation to have a proper perspective. Jesus was making a point regarding faith, and if her status and financial condition were not common knowledge, the point would have been lost to the others.

Let's look at the time leading up to this incident. Do you think she might have been in a spiritual desert, wondering every day how she was going to live and what she would eat? Where she would find shelter? She would have been worrying about everything that would consume your thoughts if you were in her circumstances. But that desert experience was necessary to provide the background that would give meaning to her action. If it were not common knowledge that she was a destitute widow with no means of support and those two small coins were everything she had in the world, throwing a couple of pennies in the collection plate would have had no meaning at all.

We will dive much deeper into this in the last chapter when we pull this all together. In the meantime, if you are in a *desert place* right now, the questions that need to be answered are: (1) Why are you there? (2) Who put you there (God or Satan)? (3) What do you need to do to move forward?

If while you are reading this you happen to be in the desert you need to spend time figuring out why. Once you know the why you can find out the how. My own particular desert times over the years have been because of guilt. My mother disciplined by guilt. Whatever I did it was what is wrong with you, what kind of a person does things like this and on and on. If yours is a guilt situation let's look again at the life of David.

One of the downfalls of David's life was his affair with Bathsheba and then the planned killing of Uriah, her husband. But when the Lord sent the prophet Nathan to rebuke David for what he had done, David instantly repented for the sin. God accepted his request for forgiveness but declared that his child born to Bathsheba would die. When the baby became sick, David sat on the floor of his bedroom and begged God to spare the child. When the infant finally died, David accepted his punishment, restored his fellowship with God, and resumed normal activity. When questioned about this, David replied that while the child was still alive, possibly the Lord would change His mind; but now that the child was dead, further prayer on his behalf would be useless.

We learn two important things about David in this story. One is that as soon as David was confronted with his sin, he repented; and two, David did not question God's decision, but accepted it and moved on. Without this attitude, David could have easily wound up in a desert situation, wondering how God could forgive his adultery and cold-blooded murder. He did, however, have to bury his son as the result of his sin. The question of who put David in the situation to begin with is obvious. God would never use a situation involving adultery and murder as a training session, so this situation came straight from the devil. It is an altogether common situation that the devil uses to this day to disrupt many lives in many ways. The point is that the two ways of dealing with guilt are try to hide it, but unfortunately you cannot hide it from yourself and you certainly can't hide it from God. David did both, he tried to hide it but when confronted by Nathan, he immediately acknowledged it and begged God for forgiveness. Once dealing with it he still had to accept the consequences of what he did but, in the end, he came out a better person and Psalm 51 would seem to indicate that his relationship with God improved.

Another thing that can lead people into a trip to the desert is not trusting God in what He wants you to do. The longer you live, the more you will probably understand that God uses a different clock than we do. We live in a world that wants everything right now – instant gratification.

Have You Ever Been Spiritually Stranded In The Desert?

Many problems of the world can be resolved in a sixty-minute television show or, worst case scenario, a two-hour movie.

When I was young, if we wanted an answer to a problem, we would often spend several hours or maybe even days going to the library to do research in several books. Now we get irritated if the Internet is slow, and it takes the computer thirty seconds to load the answer from our Google search. Going farther back in history the answers could come even slower.

When God led the children of Israel out of Egypt and through the wilderness to the Promised Land, He led them on a circuitous route. When they finally reached the Promised Land, and He ordered them to go in and take it, they resisted, saying the people there were too powerful. To paraphrase God his answer was, "Okay, if you don't want to trust Me, then you can just wander around in the desert until all the men twenty years old and older have died off, and then the next generation can claim the Promised Land."

Their desert experience clearly came from the devil. And how did Satan create this desert experience? With a total lie. Twelve men were sent to spy in the land. Ten came back saying that the people of the land were too strong for them to conquer. They cried, *Why did we not die in Egypt or in the desert?* These ten men believed a total lie, and that lie was that God was not able to deliver on his promise. That lie caused the next generation to have to wander in the desert for the next forty years.

Let's think about that. If you were just shy of twenty years old, you would have spent the next forty or so years wandering in the desert and waiting for all your elders to die. When the day finally arrived to cross the Jordan and enter the land, you would have been upwards of sixty-years old. I am sure more than one person questioned God as to how long this wandering would continue. They must have thought, *Can't they just die so we can get into the Promised Land? Just how long do we have to wait?* Here we see many people in the desert, through no fault of their own, but because of the lack of faith of others. In this particular case, those who caused the desert experience could do nothing about it, but the road sign for the next generation was clear: "When your turn comes, learn from their mistakes and do things differently." Could this desert experience have caused the next generation to have a hunger and commitment to fight for the promised land in a way that no other experience could have supplied?

Consider also the story of Jonah. God instructed him to go to Nineveh and preach, but Jonah did not want to go. Jonah hated the Ninevites and did not want to preach to them; he knew God was a forgiving God, and he did not want the Ninevites to be forgiven. Instead, Jonah boarded a ship going in the opposite direction.

A fierce storm soon arose, and everyone aboard began looking for the source of the trouble. When it was revealed that Jonah was the cause of the storm, the sailors asked him what needed to be done to save them. He told them to throw him overboard and the storm would subside. The sailors then prayed to Jonah's God not to hold them guilty and to forgive them for throwing Jonah overboard. First, God used Jonah's disobedience to introduce Himself to these sailors, and then Jonah's desert experience began in the stomach of a great fish.

In the belly of this fish, Jonah began to repent and turn back to God. Three days later, the fish beached itself and vomited Jonah onto the shore. Jonah had endured enough, so he went to Nineveh and preached as he was initially commanded to do. The Ninevites repented in sackcloth and turned to the Lord. What was Jonah's reaction to this? He turned on God again, complaining that this was why he did not want to preach to the Ninevites in the first place: because he knew this might happen. And he went out into the desert to sulk.

Jonah actually asked to die because the Ninevites repented. God addressed some choice comments to Jonah, but we are not told whether or not Jonah ever came around. The pertinent issue for our study is that Jonah wound up in his desert experience because he did not understand the mind of God and did not want to listen. How many times do we wind up in a similar situation because we believe we know better than God?

Have You Ever Been Spiritually Stranded In The Desert?

The flip side of that coin comes into view when we try to run ahead of God. We have an idea we believe has merit, so we pursue it. In that pursuit, it is possible to run ahead of God. Type A personalities are great at this. I know because, in many ways, I am a type A. It's "damn the torpedoes, full speed ahead" (Admiral Farragut was obviously a type A). At times, I have the patience of a flashbulb. I am very prone to jumping in with both feet and telling God to keep up if He can. Well, God is not going to keep up. He is not a follower; He is a leader. If He is not leading somewhere, He is not going there, and there *will* be trouble on the horizon. When that trouble inevitably comes, it may well lead to a desert experience.

It may not be a major issue at all that drives us into the desert. Just regular life can do it. It is sometimes a struggle to keep up with the job, the bills, the house, the kids, and the thousand other things that invade our minds, all of which are standing on their tiptoes and screaming at the top of their lungs when we are in bed trying to sleep. The issue is, why do we not believe God when He says He is more than willing to take the burden from us? Believe me, I am not going to chastise anyone for this, because it took three-plus years in the desert for me to learn it.

When it gets so bad that you are mentally and physically exhausted and can barely stand up, let alone move, it is a welcome relief to say, "Okay, God, it is Yours." When I finally reached that point and truly surrendered everything to God, I was set free. I quit thinking about my problem, and since I wasn't really thinking about it anymore, I wasn't worrying about it. The load was actually gone – I mean, really gone. My wife still asks me about it from time to time, wondering how I think the lawsuits will turn out – whether or not we will win, get our money back, etc. My standard response is that it is not my problem, but God's, and concerning myself with it will not change a thing. I don't know why I didn't figure this out seventy years earlier; life would have been much easier. However, I am getting into the last chapter early. We still have other things to figure out before we get there.

GOD'S *Love* LANGUAGE

Now, let's move on to how we can find out way into the desert. In the examples we examined, Jesus was there for training that he needed to complete his journey on the earth. The widow was being used by God to make a point and teach a necessary lesson. David was there because he was not where he should have been spiritually and got caught up in a lustful situation. The younger generation in the nation of Israel was there because the older generation did not trust God to deliver on his promises. Jonah was there because he *did* believe God would deliver on his promises and did not like the probable outcome. Or it may be that you believed a lie and wound up someplace you never intended.

If it proves to be Satan who put you in the desert, the solution is to go to God. If it was Satan that put you in the desert, it was undoubtedly a result of believing a lie. When Jesus was in the desert, at His lowest and weakest point, the devil came to torment Him. What did he use to torment? Lies! The devil, in an attempt to disrupt all Jesus' positive accomplishments in the forty days, the devil used lies. How did Jesus respond? He went on the offense and quoted Scripture to him.

To be fair, I believe we all would acknowledge that Jesus knew the Scriptures better than anyone who has ever lived. Nonetheless, to refute the devil and his torments, we may not have the answers on the tips of our tongues, and we may need to search the Scriptures for the answers, but they are there and, with God's help, we can find them. The desert experience is certainly not the only time that the devil will attack. Generally speaking, if we are not attempting to do something positive, there is no reason for him to try to derail us. However, there is another possibility, you may be on the verge of something noteworthy and the Devil will try to break you so that something won't happen. But in any case, the answer to any attack is time with God and his Word.

If it was, indeed, God who put us in the desert, we are there for a reason. The widow with two coins was in the desert because God needed to establish her life in preparation for her part in the lesson and example to which she was the key person. To find our reason may require a great deal of time in the Scriptures and in prayer, and even then, we may never

Have You Ever Been Spiritually Stranded In The Desert?

in this life find that reason. I wonder if the widow ever did realize what she had accomplished with her faithfulness until she got to heaven. In either case, whether we are in the desert because of Satan or because of God, the answer will be found in God's Word and in prayer. My suggestion would be to spend time in both the Old and New Testaments daily. Start in Genesis and Matthew, and read some each day. The amount is between you and God. And hang tough. We may never in this lifetime realize why we are experiencing the hard times we are going through, but be assured that there is a reason.

In my experience, if you are reading the Bible consistently and spending time communicating with God, when you need help, you will find yourself in the place where the help will be found. When God puts you in the desert, it is because He wants to get time alone with you and communicate – and it can be quite a communication. God and I had some real knockdown drag-out fights. Some of them lasted for months, and I had a lot to say to God. If you ever find yourself in that situation, be honest with God. Tell Him what is really on your mind. He is a big boy and can take it. Don't get all pious in your prayers and try to fool God, because He knows more about you than you do. If you are mad, tell Him why you are mad; if you are disappointed, tell Him why. Be brutally honest. It took me a lot of time to actually do that, but it did result in progress.

What we need to realize about desert experiences is they generally are desperate experiences. Human intelligence will generally not get you out of a desert experience; it requires the guidance of the Lord to *properly* get you out of the desert. Some may argue this, stating that human intelligence is capable of solving problems and coming up with solutions. They may point you to all the medical advances mankind has made and all the engineering problems man has solved. That being said, I can show you just as many disasters that the human mind has caused.

There is a program on TV that I watch occasionally called *Engineering Disasters*. Yes, there are enough of them to make a TV series. It demonstrates the fact that man can think his way out of problems, but he has a very real possibility of thinking himself into a worse problem. God, on the other hand, will never come up with a bad solution. His answer is always the best of all possible solutions for us. We will take a deep dive into this in the final chapters, but for the time being, just recognize that God knows the end of every fork in the road and which one will produce the best outcome.

Another reality with the desert is God may have you there waiting for something else to be ready for you. Think about Moses. After killing the Egyptian, he fled Egypt to Midian and spent years there. He took a wife, had children, and settled down. Although he was there primarily to learn, God also had him parked there until the situation in Egypt was ready for him. Once things were ready, God called him out of Midian and sent him back to Egypt.

Consider the life of Jesus. He was born and, for twelve years… *silence*. At the age of twelve, He was found in the temple discussing Scripture with the priests. Everyone was amazed at his grasp and knowledge of the Scriptures but again silence for another eighteen years. It is not that he did nothing during those years; he lived and worked and most importantly, he was a perfect child and adult. If you had a perfect child, don't you think that the people in your community would notice.

A friend might approach Mary and say, "My boy did this and I am at my wit's end. I don't know what to do." Mary could reply, "I don't know what to tell you, Jesus never did anything like that." Don't you think that his reputation got around town? It may be that your job right now is just to be the best, kindest and most thoughtful person possible so others can notice.

It may be that God has parked you in a desert situation until other circumstances line up, and then, because of your particular skill set, He will give you your instructions. This is another reason you do not want to move until God says to move. This requires time spent in the Bible and time spent in prayer. If you do not take this time, you will have a difficult time knowing what God has in mind. In my experience, reading the Bible, along with prayer, have been absolutely necessary to

Have You Ever Been Spiritually Stranded In The Desert?

accomplish a positive outcome. They are the primary way that we can obtain the kind of Godly wisdom needed to handle whatever comes up. Could Jesus have defeated the Devils lies without the godly wisdom that came from scripture? Keep in mind at that time, Jesus was in a completely human state. He had willingly put aside all of His divine powers. As you read of his ministry it is obvious that he accomplished everything he did through God the Father and he was continuously quoting scripture as he taught. Now I am not saying that it is impossible for God to speak to us directly; God has, on numerous occasions, put a thought in my mind regarding something, but in my case, it has always been bringing to mind Scripture that I had read. My mother-in-law was saved as a result of a dream. Others I have heard of have had the experience of god imparting some kind of wisdom by direct revelation. But if you are desperate for answers, the most direct way to find them is to be proactive by spending time with God in his Word and prayer.

Finally, do not fear or avoid a desert experience. Do not look for a shortcut out of it, because a desert experience is always there to teach you something you would not be able to learn otherwise.

Chapter 6
WHAT DOES GOD THINK WE SHOULD DO?

To answer this chapter's question, again an examination of the life of David is in order. God, throughout Scripture, refers to David as being a man after His own heart. What was it about David that would make God think of him in that way?

Before I delve into David and his relationship with God, I need to insert a disclaimer. I do not, in any way, want to foster the idea that all mental problems can be solved with Bible study and prayer. I spent part of my life in a very legalistic church that did not believe in therapy. They believed that if you were right with God, He would fix any problem with your mind. I want to be perfectly clear that some problems absolutely need the assistance of a qualified therapist and possibly medication, and I urge you, if you need outside help, by all means, get it. What I will discuss in this chapter are those problems that put us into a tailspin, but not to the point of mental illness.

Having said that, we meet David in 1 Samuel 16, when Samuel anointed him king. One by one the sons of Jesse were paraded in front of Samuel. When Samuel saw Eliab, he thought, *Surely this was the one*, but God told him not to look at his appearance because He looks at the heart. When all of Jesse's sons who were present had passed in front of Samuel, the Lord told him none of these were the one.

Samuel then asked if there were any more sons and was informed there was another, the youngest, but he was tending sheep. Then Jesse sent someone for David, and when Samuel saw him, God said he was the one. In response, Samuel anointed David. After his anointing, David went back to tending sheep because he had to wait for the events to unfold that would ultimately place him on the throne.

We next see David when he entered Saul's service as a musician to calm the king when he was troubled by an evil spirit. After God rejected Saul as king and instructed Samuel to anoint David, the Holy Spirit was taken from Saul. Without the Holy Spirit to calm and guide him, Saul became given to violent outbursts and paranoia. It must have become well known in the palace because Saul's advisors suggested they find someone who could soothe him with music. One of Saul's advisors had heard of David and must have been impressed enough to recommend him. David was sent for, and after his "audition," he was hired. Saul was so taken with David that in addition to his duties as a musician, he was made one of Saul's armor-bearers. This apparently was not a full-time position, because we are told that David traveled between the palace and his home.

Next, we see David and Goliath, undoubtedly the most well-known story about David. There was war between Israel and the Philistines. The armies lined up on opposing hills, Israel on one hill and the Philistines on another, with a valley in between. Every day Goliath would come out and challenge Israel to send a man to fight with him. If the Israelite won, then the Philistines would be Israel's servants, but if Goliath won, then Israel would be the Philistines' servants. Jesse sent David to take some food and supplies to his brothers, who were in the army. Just as David entered the camp, Goliath was issuing this challenge again, as he had done morning and evening for forty days. When David heard the challenge, his response was, "Who is this uncircumcised Philistine to defy the living God?" David did not care that this man was over nine feet tall and a trained warrior. He only saw that he was defying God.

David approached Saul and offered to face Goliath. Saul looked at the young man before him and questioned how he planned to do this. Saul knew David as a musician and a shepherd but certainly not as a warrior. I can hear the sneer in Saul's voice as he asked David how he

What Does God Think We Should Do?

intended to kill this giant and lifelong trained warrior. David's answer was that while tending his father's sheep, he had fought a lion and a bear to protect the sheep. I suspect that more than one lion and bear had come across his path, and God had used them to prepare David for Goliath. In this conversation with Saul, David went on to say that the same God who had helped him with the lion and the bear would help him defeat Goliath.

I have often thought about David with the flock, seeing a lion or bear approaching and saying to himself, *Again?* But I digress.

David *ran* out to meet Goliath; he was so excited and confident in God that he ran out to face his foe and once again see God at work. It only recently dawned on me that David was not even fully equipped to face Goliath when he began running toward him. He obviously did not yet have any ammunition for his sling, because when he crossed the stream that ran through the valley, he stopped to pick out five smooth river stones. Why five stones? Maybe because Goliath had four brothers?

Nevertheless, when David accepted the challenge of Goliath, he did not stop to think about how he was going to handle the situation. He just went forward believing that God was with him and he did not have to worry about anything. And not only did he go, but he *ran* to meet the challenge. Additionally, he must have known he did not have any stones, but he obviously did not worry about it. He simply believed that if God had given him the challenge, then God would provide the means. All he needed to do was show up.

Another consideration is that the means David needed to accomplish his task was nothing more than a smooth river stone—a *river stone*, something so common you can find thousands of them in any river or stream in the world. Generally, you do not need anything exotic to accomplish God's purpose, just something that happens to be lying around you. Many times I have heard someone say, in one form or another, "If I only had _____, I could do great things for God." In reality, maybe all we need is a smooth stone from the bed of the river we are crossing.

When Goliath saw David approaching, he cursed and ridiculed him by his gods and said he would feed him to the birds. David's response to Goliath was he might be coming with sword and spear, but he (David) was coming in the power of the God of Israel. God would deliver Goliath into his hand, and David said he would cut his head off that day. We see from these words that David did not question God when God put a difficult situation in front of him. He believed God and ran to meet the challenge in the power of God. That is instantaneous obedience without thinking of possible consequences. David thought nothing about himself but jumped at every chance to serve God.

David's defeat of Goliath made him a national hero, and this caused Saul's rage and paranoia to reach epidemic proportions. Saul began trying to kill David. Jonathan, Saul's son, talked him out of it on several occasions, but eventually, David and his men had to flee from Saul, who was in hot pursuit with the Israelite army. On two occasions, David had the opportunity to kill Saul. Had David done it, I can imagine the hundreds of sermons that would have been preached about living for God and seeing Him put your enemies at your feet and give you victory over them.

The men with David encouraged him to put an end to Saul, declaring that God had delivered his enemy to him. David, however, refused to touch Saul, saying he would not put his hands on God's anointed. David knew beyond a shadow of a doubt that God had rejected Saul, and he had been anointed king, but still, David regarded Saul as God's anointed. Since God had made Saul king, it was God's job to remove him, even if it meant David had to continue to live in jeopardy. That's another insight into the mind of David.

David and his men continued to run and hide from Saul. In spite of his circumstances, David persisted in fighting the enemies of Israel, keeping up the good fight, and again doing what God had equipped him for. Eventually, in a war with the Philistines, Saul and Jonathan were killed. After their deaths, David and his men mourned for them, giving the king and his son the respect David felt they deserved.

What Does God Think We Should Do?

Shortly after this, David inquired of God whether he should go up to Judah. God told him to go, and David was then installed as king over Judah. In the Northern Kingdom, Ish-Bosheth, son of Saul, was anointed king over Israel. This divided kingdom created war between the house of David and the house of Saul for several years, but eventually, Israel was defeated. The Northern and Southern Kingdoms were reunited, and David became king over both.

David did what he was best at and defeated Israel's enemies. In one of the battles, David conquered Jerusalem and took up residence there, calling it the City of David. David set up his palace in Jerusalem, and from there, he continued to battle their enemies. With God's help, he defeated them all. The gold and silver taken from these enemies was dedicated to God.

David wanted to build a temple in Jerusalem, but God sent the prophet Nathan to tell him that he was not the one to build the temple, but that it would be his son who would build it. This did not discourage David. Even though he was not the one to build the temple, he took it upon himself to stockpile materials so they would be available for the building when it went up.

Now we will look at the worst time in David's life. The army had gone to war, but David stayed home. David saw Bathsheba and became enamored with her. He inquired about her and learned she was the wife of Uriah, one of his chief fighting men. With no thought of consequences, David sent for Bathsheba and slept with her. That short affair resulted in a pregnancy. In an attempt to cover this up, David sent for Uriah to "inquire how the battle was going." In reality, he was hoping Uriah would go to his house and sleep with his wife. Uriah, being a much more honorable man than David, refused to go home, asserting that it would be wrong for him to go home and be comforted by his wife while all the others in the army were out fighting.

Because Uriah would not "cooperate," David gave a letter to Uriah that he was to deliver to the army commander. This letter instructed the commander to place Uriah in the hottest part of the battle and then to draw back from him. Understand this – David was so caught up in his sin that he actually had Uriah carry his own death sentence to the army commander! This is the same man whom the Bible referred to as a man after God's own heart.

In the Saturday morning Bible study I attend, we recently studied the life of David. If you read his life carefully, you will see he was perfect for the job God called him to do. That job was to conquer all of Israel's enemies. He was great at it, a fearless and cunning warrior and leader of men. His problem was he did not know how to behave in civilian life. He was not a great father; his kids did all kinds of wrong things. One of his sons, Amnon, raped his half-sister Tamar. David, even though he was furious when he heard of it, apparently did nothing about it. As a result, Tamar's brother Absalom plotted against Amnon and eventually killed him. After killing Amnon, Absalom fled to Geshur, where he stayed for three years. Eventually, David allowed Absalom to return to Jerusalem, where he and David were reunited, but we are not told that David ever did anything to Absalom for killing his brother.

Absalom then began plotting a coup to take the kingdom away from David. He seized control of the army and tried to hunt his father down and kill him. When Absalom was killed in battle, instead of commending his troops for the victory and rejoicing with them, David loudly mourned the loss of his son. Had it not been for the counsel of Joab, David may well have lost the support of his army. Joab admonished David that his behavior made it seem that David would have been more pleased if his whole army had died, and Absalom had lived. Heeding Joab's words, David sat in the gateway and made amends with his troops.

Later, over the protests of his advisors, David ordered the army to be numbered, in direct contradiction to God's wishes, putting the nation in jeopardy of God's wrath. On and on go the accounts of David's misdeeds.

At the end of one of our studies, one of the group members voiced what we all probably thought at one time or another in our study of David's life: how can this man represent a man after God's own heart?

What Does God Think We Should Do?

That's a really good question. It was one I pondered all the next week. Finally, near the end of the week, I thought of an answer.

Yes, David did a lot of dumb things and committed some really deplorable sins. But at the end of the day, when David realized his sin, he immediately repented—I mean, he really repented. Read Psalms 32 and 51, psalms written after his affair with Bathsheba. David made no excuses; he did not offer any kind of mitigating circumstances, but merely said, *"For I know my transgressions and my sin is always before me. Against you and you only have I sinned and done what is evil in your sight"* (Ps. 51:3–4). When David acknowledged his sin, he did so without reservation. In every case, God accepted David's repentance, and in God's sight, that sin was forgotten. Of course, David still had to suffer the consequences of his sin, but when God looked at David, He saw only the good and none of the bad.

Another person I would like to examine in this context is Samson. One of the unexpected names to appear in God's *Who's Who* in Hebrews 11 is Samson. When you read Samson's story in the book of Judges, you learn he was a Nazarite from birth. This meant that Samson was to live a much more restrictive lifestyle than the average Hebrew. However, as you read his story, you see he was anything but an "altar boy." Nonetheless, like David, when God gave Samson a job to do, he took God along with him all the way. It is clearly stated in the account of his life that his remarkable feats and his tremendous strength were products of having God in his life. However, when it came to his personal life, like David, Samson was a mess.

David and Samson were unquestionably men of God. David is described as a man after God's own heart, and Samson is mentioned in God's *Who's Who*. There are numerous similarities between the two men. Samson was a judge during the time of the judges, which made him a leader in the land, and David was Israel's second king. Both men warred with the Philistines, David with a conventional army, and Samson as a one-man army. They both were victorious over the Philistines.

The main difference I see between the two is that David, who played a much bigger role in God's plan than did Samson, quickly repented for the horrendous sins he committed in his personal life, while Samson did not seem to have that kind of conscience. Though Samson continued to wreak havoc on the Philistines, which was his job, his personal life remained a mess.

Eventually, he took up with a prostitute named Delilah. Delilah nagged Samson relentlessly until he revealed to her the secret of his strength. Once she knew, she cut off his hair so that he lost his strength. The Philistines then captured him, gouged out his eyes, and shackled him to a grinding stone, using him as a beast of burden.

Over time, Samson's hair grew back, unnoticed by the Philistines, and one day he was taken to the temple of Dagon for sport. He asked to be positioned between the supporting columns, where he prayed to God. However, his prayer was not one of repentance, but of vengeance. Samson asked God to give him his strength back so he could bring the temple down and kill the Philistines to repay them for blinding him. In spite of this, we find Samson in the eleventh chapter of Hebrews.

The common denominator in the stories of these two men seems to be that in spite of all they did wrong when they performed the task God gave them, they did it completely in the strength and power of God – fully trusting, fully committed, and fully faithful.

So how does this translate to today? While the particulars of our lives are worlds apart from the lives of David and Samson, the lessons are the same. Are we going to encounter problems? Absolutely. Are some of those problems going to be larger than life? Probably. Can we approach those problems with the same attitude that David and Samson did? Why not? God has not changed.

In John 15, Jesus talks about being the vine while we are the branches. If a branch bears no fruit, it is cut off, but if a branch does bear fruit, it is pruned to become even more fruitful. The lesson is clear: if you choose to serve God, He will bring situations into your life for training. The purpose of the training is to prune that which is harmful to your obedience. In other words, God will put you in certain situations to help you get rid of something, or to learn something.

The way God generally works is to challenge us at our strong points with the objective of making us realize our pride. The goal is to have us realize that what we consider our strong points are really weak points for His service. Because we are too confident in our strong points, we often forge ahead and do not seek His guidance.

In studying David's life, we see he endured many attacks from the devil at his weak points, and he indeed had an abundance of weak points. But in every case, the devil was unsuccessful in his attempts to derail David from God's plan because David was always ready to repent. He did not want to wind up in the desert.

David took to heart the problems God sent his way for instruction and training. He always took God along whenever God had something for him to do.

David, here comes a lion! "Come along, God. With You, a lion is nothing."

What about that bear? "Come along, God. We need to save the flock from the bear."

There's the giant Goliath! "Come along, God. We need to teach him and the Philistines some respect for You."

What will you do about Saul? "No, God, I will not touch him, as I consider him Your anointed. If You want him gone, You will need to do it."

As king, David asked God, "Should I attack the Philistines. Yes? Okay, God, let's do this."

What made David a man after God's heart was that God never needed to break David's pride. No matter the job assigned to him, the first contact he made was with God. He never tried to do anything for God in his own strength. Additionally, despite the many dumb things David did, as soon as he realized he had done wrong, he repented. If you want an understanding of the mind of David, start reading at Psalm 15 and just keep going. Psalm 18, in particular, shows David's humility in his relationship with God.

I do not know whether or not you have ever been around a flock of sheep. If you have, you will know what I am talking about; if not, just believe me that sheep are really dumb. A shepherd does not lead a very exciting life. About all the shepherd needs to do is to keep moving the sheep to places where they can graze. It is not rocket science, and it does not take a great deal of complicated knowledge to shepherd sheep. But David did not take the job lightly; he included God in every part of the task.

So how do we apply David to our lives? I don't tend sheep; neither do I anticipate meeting a lion or a bear in the suburbs. I doubt that at my age I will be joining the army and facing a Goliath anytime soon, so how does this apply? Okay, no lions or bears, but what about a financial crisis, an accident, or a medical emergency? There are two ways to look at them. We can look at it with human understanding and ask, "Why did this happen to me, God?" Or we can look at it David's way and say, "Let's go, God. How are we going to battle this? The odds look insurmountable, but with You at my side, nothing is too big. Oh, I am crossing a stream and those smooth river stones are just the right size for my sling; one of these stones is marked for Goliath."

Does this mean we will win every battle? I can definitely state without reservation that every battle we enter with God at our side will result in a victory of one kind or another.

An entire book could be written to cover all the issues we might possibly encounter in life. Let it suffice to say that from the smallest irritant to the largest crisis, the solution is the same. The first contact must be God. Think of David. He did not worry about how well-equipped he was for the job; he just put his hand into God's and followed Him, believing God would supply the means on the way: "I need to teach Goliath and the Philistines some respect. How do I do this, God? Oh, here is a streambed, and these smooth river stones are perfect for my sling." Don't look at your Goliath as being too big to fight, but rather look at him as being too big to miss.

And what about Samson? What can we learn from him? Face any problem with all the strength you have and rely on God to supply the strength you do not have. Samson, facing the Philistine army alone, prayed, "God, give me strength; I have no weapon. OK, God. Here is the jawbone of a donkey. I can use that to kill a thousand Philistines."

Our problems may be completely different, but God is the same, and the same principle applies: God + 1 = a majority.

To wrap this all up in a few sentences, God has a job for every believer. He will equip you for whatever that job is. He will send the Holy Spirit along with you to protect and guide, or comfort and console. That job, no matter how insignificant you may think it to be, plays a critical role in the overall picture. Once you have completed that job, you will gain a reward for it in heaven, and that reward will be with you for all eternity.

Our existence does not consist of the things of this world. They are there sometimes for our comfort and sometimes for us to use in service to God. Our existence is meant to find our place in God's plan and fulfill it.

Let me end this chapter where I began. Many of you will be driven into a state of depression over circumstances, as I have been on many occasions. I do not want to imply as I relate to these biblical figures that God is going to magically change everything. He still has not changed anything in my life, but he has through Bible study and prayer, *and* sometimes therapy and, on certain occasions, medications, taught me how to deal with it. It has resulted in my ability to look at things from God's perspective and believe he will produce a favorable result. I still struggle with it, but not nearly as much as before. So, if you are in a bad place and you can't handle it, get help. Also, keep communicating with God and the answers will come.

Chapter 7
WHAT IS GOD'S PLANNED RESULT?

Congratulations to those of you who have stuck with me to this, the last chapter. We are now going to take a deep dive into what God's love is all about.

Ephesians 2:10 says, *"For we are God's workmanship, created in Christ Jesus to do good works, which God prepared in advance for us to do."* This, in a nutshell, is our purpose in being here. We are told in Jeremiah, *"Before I formed you in the womb, I knew you; before you were born, I set you apart."* God has a destiny for each and every one of us to serve Him in a very special way that no one else on earth is capable of doing. That is because no one else on earth has been exactly where we have been, seen what we have seen, experienced what we have experienced, and done what we have done. The totality of our lives has been choreographed by God.

Your immediate reaction might be, *Wait a minute. I thought I had free will and freedom of choice.* You do, but before you were saved, God encouraged you through the situations you experienced to accept Christ and be born again. After that decision, God either placed or allowed circumstances in your life in an attempt to direct you to the service you were made for. In either case, you have had the option to obey and follow, or ignore and miss out on the blessings God has in store for us.

We have previously taken a brief look into Moses' life, but let's take a closer review. God decided that Moses would be the one to lead the nation of Israel out of Egypt and into the Promised Land. Moses, however, was born at a time when all male Jewish babies were thrown into the Nile River. God directed Moses' mother to build a small boat, in which she placed Moses. She instructed Miriam, Moses' sister, to place it in the river, where the baby was found by Pharaoh's daughter. God softened her heart and, taking pity on Moses, she took him into her home, which was Pharaoh's home.

Moses was raised as a son of Pharaoh and taught all the principles of royal leadership. He learned how to properly train people under his command to accomplish a task. He learned how to recognize and use people for the tasks they were best suited to do. He learned how to encourage when it was warranted, to discipline when it was needed. He learned the necessity of hard decisions. In short, he was trained to be a pharaoh himself.

At some point, Moses realized he was an Israelite and forsook the luxury of being Pharaoh's son, aligning himself with his own people. When he saw an Egyptian mistreating an Israelite, he came to their defense and killed the Egyptian. When his crime was discovered, he fled for his life and wound up in Midian, on the backside of the desert and tending sheep. After his leadership training in the house of Pharaoh, he spent the next forty years tending sheep.

His leadership training now required another facet. Moses had to learn how to lead people who were not necessarily willing to follow. There is no better training ground for that than tending sheep. Sheep are incredibly stupid animals and, left to their own devices, they will wind up in trouble almost 100 percent of the time. By the end of all his training, Moses had a college degree in teaching the teachable and another degree in herding the masses. He was perfectly suited for the task God laid out for him.

I would now like to turn your attention to the widow who put the two small coins into the collection plate. As we discussed before, her training for her task was to survive widowhood and all that went along with it. She was destitute, alone, with no means of generating income and no way out of her plight. On top of all this, she was asked to give

What Is God's Planned Result?

up all the money she had in the world. Both she and Moses had the free will to say no to God. The widow could have reasoned that her two small coins would not do any good and that it was all she had to spend for her next meal. Moses could have said to God, "I have made a life for myself here. I have a wife and family. Besides, You abandoned me here for forty years, and now You want me back?" Fortunately, neither disappointed God, and both accomplished the task God laid out for them. The reason for this is that both were willing to communicate with God.

In both cases, had they not followed God's lead, millions of people would have missed out on something good. In the case of Moses, around two million people needed God's guidance to leave Egypt and enter the Promised Land. Over the years, millions more have been influenced or encouraged by God's deliverance and guidance of the Hebrew nation. In the case of the widow, only a handful of people witnessed the initial act, but over the next two thousand years, millions have been encouraged and instructed in properly handling whatever God has entrusted to them.

The important point is our decisions can affect an unknown number of people. Moses obviously knew that his decisions would affect a lot of people, but he may not have realized the exodus would become one of the most important events in the history of Israel. Without him, it may not have transpired correctly, or at all. If you read the Old Testament, you see that time and again, the exodus is recalled to remind people of the greatness of God. I seriously doubt that the widow held any illusions that her act of selfless giving would become the center point of countless sermons and a source of encouragement and comfort to many people going through hard times. Likewise, we do not have any idea what the ramifications will be of our decisions.

Every decision we make affects someone around us, either knowingly or unknowingly. It can go either way, good or bad, depending upon what we do with what God asks us to do. It can be frightening to imagine the negative effect of a wrong decision on those around us. Inversely, it can be incredibly exciting to watch God work with something we handled correctly. The reality is we will probably never know in this lifetime the full consequences of our decisions, either good or bad. Regardless, never forget there are no small jobs in God's plan. In any decision, we have the same opportunity for service, but we must be in the right frame of mind.

There is a quality that seems to be all but lost in the Christian community, and that is the spirit of holiness or godliness. Second Peter 1:5–8 explains we have the ability to acquire holiness, but it requires effort. We must pursue goodness, knowledge, self-control, perseverance, godliness, brotherly kindness, and love. If we possess these qualities in increasing measure, we will be productive in God's kingdom. However, the implication is obvious, that without these qualities, we will be unproductive or, at the very best, much less productive than we could be.

Also, note we need these traits in increasing measure. In other words, it is a lifestyle; we do not acquire these traits and then have them for the rest of our lives. No! We must work at them, constantly improving. No one ever became a highly successful anything without a lot of hard work. I have heard it said that oftentimes, when opportunity comes knocking at the front door, it is not recognized because it comes disguised as hard work.

Proverbs 8 speaks much about wisdom, its value, and the potential effect on our lives. Throughout the chapter, we are encouraged to seek it. The book of Proverbs also tells us the fear of the Lord is the beginning of wisdom. I believe much misunderstanding exists about the fear of the Lord. In this book, we have completed six chapters largely about the negatives of this life, which demonstrate our view of the Lord. On the positive side, as simply as I can state it, the fear of the Lord is simply recognizing who He is.

Recall His great power, with a spoken word He created the universe. Reflect on His great mercy, He was willing to endure the crucifixion so we could become His brothers and sisters forever in heaven. Remember His great justice; someday, we will see Him pass judgment on every wrong that has been perpetrated against Him or us. Think about His great comfort; if we allow Him, He will be our guide and comfort us through every problem and trial.

Once we have learned to fear the Lord—or possibly more accurate in today's English, once we put Him in proper perspective, giving Him the proper place in our thinking—only then will we possess the right frame of mind to pursue wisdom and gain holiness. These two attributes are absolutely necessary for our spiritual growth, and our spiritual growth is absolutely critical in properly accomplishing our divine purpose.

Psalm 49:16–20 is the antithesis of a godly life and attitude. We are told not to be impressed with the rich because they will take nothing with them when they die. Their splendor will not follow them to the grave. However, the Bible tells us with absolute certainty that eternal reward follows obedience to God. Let's go back to Moses and the widow. They have been enjoying their reward for a long time now and will enjoy it for the rest of eternity. I do not believe Moses received any more reward than the unnamed widow, because both successfully completed their assigned tasks.

I was recently listening to a Christian radio station and heard the remark that Christianity seems to be developing into a Bible-less relationship. Sadly, a large number of Christians today almost never read their Bibles. They go to church and listen to the pastor, even taking notes and writing down a few references, but they have no set schedule of Bible reading, if they even read it at all. How well do you think you would do at your job if you had absolutely no communication with your boss? How well do you think your marriage would do if there was no communication? How well do you think your kids would turn out if you never communicated with them? No relationship can be built without communication. By what stretch of the imagination can we build a relationship with God, let alone have any idea of what He wants us to do, without the proper communication?

I have mentioned I went into a business venture that went terribly wrong. If it were not that I was established in the habit of reading my Bible and praying to start almost every morning, I have no idea where

I would have wound up. But the time I spent in the Bible positioned my mind in a positive direction and ultimately resulted in the writing of this book. I have no idea what this book might accomplish, but all the Bible study, meditation, and prayer that went into it has changed my life forever.

Over the years, I have heard all the excuses, and even used most of them myself, about why a person does not read the Bible. I really don't understand it. How much did you understand math, history, reading, or any other subject at your first introduction to it? However, the more you learned about it, the more sense it made. That is how it is with the Bible. The more time you spend with it, the more sense it makes.

How about the excuse "I just don't have the time"? When was the last time you missed your favorite television show or sports event on TV? There is an answer for every excuse we can come up with for why we do not spend time with God, but the truth of the matter is we will always make the time for what we want to do.

The nuts and bolts message of this chapter is that God is working on an extremely complex tapestry, and every one of us has the opportunity to be part of it. Think about a large intricate tapestry with a thread that is the wrong color, in the wrong place, or even missing. Once you notice the mistake, you cannot take your eyes off it. Every time you look at the tapestry, you are immediately drawn to the mistake. How much of God's tapestry will be blemished because of what we chose not to do or to do incorrectly? The most beautiful things of this world will someday cease to exist, but God's tapestry will be on display forever.

How many times might we look at the tapestry and have to admit the blemish right there is because of our unwillingness to obey? This leads us to the exciting part because this is the first example of God's love that we will look at. Remarkably, God does not see the blemishes. He does not expect us to be perfect, and that is a good thing because in this life we never will be. God forgave us for our shortcomings before we ever did them.

What Is God's Planned Result?

The best example I can provide that illustrates this is the life of Samson. He was anything but the holy Nazarite he was born to be. He was a womanizer, and he broke his Nazarite vows in countless ways. In his day, the judge of the land was supposed to be the leader of the people, both legally and spiritually. Samson was neither. He was just a one-man killing machine. There is little mention of Samson ever seeking the Lord's guidance, and his last prayer mentioned was the one asking for revenge on the Philistines.

Samson's life was not one you would want to emulate, yet he is listed in verse 32 of God's Who's Who in the eleventh chapter of Hebrews. In my mind, he is the last person I would expect to find there. God, however, looked only at what Samson did right; and when he was doing God's will in eradicating the Philistines, he did it with all his might. There is no telling what Samson might have accomplished if he had lived a different life, but he was recognized and rewarded for what he did right and forgiven for what he did wrong. And so it is with us. In His love, God does not expect perfection, but He has things He wants us to do; and like Samson, Moses, the widow, we will be recognized and rewarded for whatever we accomplish for Him.

Paul's letter to the Philippians is a good read about what we need to be to accomplish God's purpose in our lives. A synopsis of the letter starts in 1:6, where Paul reflects on his confidence that God would complete the work He started in them, because of their partnership in the gospel. In verse 9, his prayer was that they would abound more and more in knowledge so they would have the ability to discern what is best, and remain pure and blameless for the day of Christ. In verse 29, Paul states that the Philippians (and we) had been granted the privilege not only to believe in Christ, but also to suffer for Him. He concludes chapter 1 with a challenge for the Philippians to conduct themselves in a manner worthy of the gospel.

Chapters 2, 3, and 4 are a list of the things we should constantly strive for:

GOD'S *Love* LANGUAGE

- Emulate the humility of Christ.
- Continue working out your own salvation.
- No grumbling or arguing.
- Pay attention to the teachers he is sending.
- Rejoice in the lord.
- Be careful of leaders that are too impressed with themselves.
- Again rejoice, don't be anxious or worry but instead pray with thanksgiving.
- Finally, think on good things, not bad or worrisome things.
- If you are in a troubled place, it would be a good book to study.

How does this translate to our service? Well, the times are different, but the principles still apply. We need to have a partnership in the gospel. Our primary concern should be to live a life that reflects our Christian status. Decisions should be made with eternity in mind. We need to pursue humility with our whole being. Pride and arrogance do not impress God; in fact, He hates them.

We need to work out our own salvation. That does not mean we can earn a ticket to heaven; for that, we can only trust the finished work of Christ by confessing our sins, asking for forgiveness, and accepting Christ. The salvation spoken of here is the constant transformation of our minds and bodies from their inborn sinful nature to something God can use for His purpose. In so doing, we will have the ability to stand out and be different in an eternal way.

We need to rejoice in the Lord, regardless of the circumstances. If we truly are searching for God's purpose in our lives, we must acknowledge there will be suffering. The purpose of suffering is to mold us into the people we need to be in order to accomplish what we need to do. I have often used Joni Eareckson Tada as an example of this because hers is one of the most severe cases I know of. Was it not for the diving accident that turned her into a quadriplegic, would her worldwide ministry exist? I do not think so. So yes, in bad times—even in those terrible, gut-wrenching times where you can barely breathe—*rejoice*! Yes, I did say, in

What Is God's Planned Result?

the most terrible times you may experience, rejoice. In those times, God knows that with His help, you can survive it and thrive at the end of it. This is one of the most difficult lessons I have learned.

Whatever we accomplish in our secular lives is meaningless to our service to God. Paul describes it as garbage. This life is nothing in light of eternity. Almost everyone reading this book probably has thought about retirement. Maybe you are already there, or maybe you are working toward it. Maybe you have a savings account, a stock portfolio, some rental income, a 401(k), or any number of other provisions aimed toward retirement. The reality, however, is any plan you have for this world will eventually end, and all you have worked for will be gone or left in someone else's hands.

The old saying you can't take it with you is one of the truest statements the world has ever made. At my age, I have attended more than a few funerals, and I can state without reservation I have never seen a hearse with a trailer hitch. Everything in this world will someday cease to exist, but the next world will last forever. Why not build up your heavenly 401(k)? You will have that for eternity.

That is precisely what Paul is talking about: working to win the prize of your service. Think of it this way. Almost everything you have belongs to God. He made this earth, and whatever is in it belongs to Him. The only thing you can claim as truly belonging to you is your time. It is yours to use any way you choose. It is also the only thing you can truly give to God. Any time spent doing God's will is time for which you will receive a reward. Paul gave up his whole life to become a homeless traveling pastor, evangelist, and missionary, but imagine his heavenly retirement.

Finally, Paul once again encourages us to rejoice in the Lord, and following that admonition is a list of things to occupy our minds with. Read that list carefully and notice what is missing: worry, fear, material comforts, concern over the state of the nation or who is in office, and a whole host of other things. Instead of all the negative concerns we seem

GOD'S *Love* LANGUAGE

to dwell on, why not dwell on the positives of God? By doing so, the God of peace will be with us.

I have reached the point where I have actually put that into practice. The last time I spoke with my attorney concerning the lawsuit, the news was all bad. I actually went into a slump for two or three hours, but then God's voice whispered in my mind and said, "This is the best news you could get. I do My best work with the impossible." Every time I think of it, I smile.

In my experience, both personally and in speaking with other people, the main reason most people are hesitant to give their lives to God and trust Him for the results is that they are scared of where God might want to put them. *Does God want me to be a missionary to Africa or South America? Does He want me to give up everything I have and run a mission in the worst part of town? Does He_____?* You fill in the blank of the worst possible thing God could ask you to do.

The reality, however, is God wants you to be in the place that will make you the happiest in His service. If you are in a job you hate, you will be lousy at it. If, on the other hand, you love what you are doing, you will probably be great at it. Here is some good news: if you can honestly say to God, "My life is Yours to do with whatever You want," then you are exactly where God wants you to be. You do not have to change a thing in your life, except, possibly, your attitude. If God wants you someplace else, He has all the ability to put you there. Think of Joseph in the Old Testament; he went from prison to the second-most powerful person in the known world in one day. Talk about an instant transformation!

When I am driving, oftentimes, I listen to the local Christian radio station. Today I heard a speaker reflecting on a flight he had recently taken. The plane experienced a mechanical problem that was discovered only after the passengers had boarded and the plane had left the terminal. The plane had to turn around, and all the passengers were required to disembark so that the problem could be corrected. The repair wound up taking an extended period of time, and by the time everyone was

What Is God's Planned Result?

back on board and they were in the air, the flight attendants were in the unenviable position of dealing with a plane full of angry passengers. They began to hand out free drinks, extra bags of pretzels or peanuts, and anything else they thought might calm the situation.

This speaker was watching one of the flight attendants who was "taking it right on the chin," as he put it. No matter how a passenger treated her, she maintained a big smile and exhibited unending grace. After they had been in flight for a while and things had settled down, the speaker on the radio program said he walked to the galley to chat with her. He asked for her name because he wanted to write a letter to the airline, commending her for her attitude and action in an extremely difficult time. Her answer to him was that she did not work for the airline, but for Jesus Christ, and she was living up to His standard. Will she receive a reward for her actions that day? You bet. You don't need to be a Paul or Peter to serve the Lord; you can do it every day in the little things you encounter.

In all probability, if you are the average Christian going through life with one foot in God's world and one foot in the secular world, initially, He will just want you to get both feet into His world. That will merely require you to change your focus on what you regard as important. To paraphrase Jesus in Matthew 6:33, put your focus on the kingdom of God and let God put His focus on your needs.

If you truly want to be where God wants you to be, I can give you the formula. Do like that flight attendant. Give every moment of every day to God. As you spend time in Bible study and prayer, you will begin to develop insight into the mind of God. As that insight grows, apply it to your life. I suspect that for most Christians, this will be the entirety of their calling, simply living a life that reflects a Christlike attitude. It may mean helping a friend or neighbor in distress or giving a little more when a need arises. Stopping whatever you are doing when God has someone in need pass in front of you. Do you think that it might have helped that flight attendant, after getting beat up from the front of that plane to the rear, to have someone walk up to her and say, "Good job"?

GOD'S *Love* LANGUAGE

When your job, spouse, kids, or someone else is driving you crazy, instead of reacting in a normal human way, counter with an understanding, godly response. In other words, apply the same kindness and understanding to everything in your life that Jesus has given to you. There was a slogan a while back that caught on for a while: WWJD, meaning what would Jesus do? It is a little simplistic, but entirely applicable. Like that flight attendant, respond with true concern for the lives and feelings of those in your life, and if God wants more of you, you will know as you read the Bible and pray.

So, what have we seen so far about God's love? First, God does not concern Himself with what we may or may not think is important to our comfort in this life. If you are a parent, you will experience many times in raising your children when you must say no to some request because you know it is not what they need. It may actually be harmful or cause them to move in a direction that will not be beneficial. When God says no to us, it is out of love because He is molding us to become what He needs us to be and protecting us from the world around us.

God extends His love to us by prompting us to trust in Jesus for our eternal security. To fully appreciate that statement, it is necessary to reflect on what it cost God to watch His Son carry the sin debt of the world and become the epitome of sinful man – in fact, so sinful that God had to turn His back on Jesus because, in His holiness, He was unable to look on all that sin. Additionally, Jesus had to endure incredible pain and torment and watch His Father turn His back on Him. All this was the most incredible act of love the world will ever see.

God helps us and encourages us in numerous ways so we can become the best-equipped servants possible to accomplish our tasks for Him. He gives us the Holy Spirit to help, guide, and direct us to a fuller understanding of what we need to correct. Of course, we have the free will to accept or decline, but Hebrews 12:7 cautions us to endure hardship as discipline so that we may share in His holiness (verse 10). That would mean our first stop is boot camp. That boot camp will mean many things to many people. That boot camp may last for days, weeks, or maybe many years. We know that Moses did not start his designated work until he was eighty. Once we express our willingness, God will work with us one-on-one to train us for whatever purpose he has in mind.

Next, He puts into our lives everything we need to accomplish that purpose. We need to understand that God does not lavish physical trinkets on those He loves. Sometimes the job He gives us is very painful. If you read Hebrews 11, you will notice that God's Who's Who starts with a list of the biggies and, up to the first half of verse 35, reflects on many who gained great victories. The second half of verse 35, however, speaks of those who were tortured and killed. In our minds, this does not indicate victory, and our natural inclination is to wonder if God loved the victorious ones more than He loved the ones who suffered torture and death. Absolutely not! If anything, He loved them more because He could trust them to remain faithful through the worst of all situations. In His love, He awarded them a martyr's crown to wear throughout eternity.

What you need to accomplish your purpose is what you have. If you have something you don't need, He can take it away. If there is something you do need, He can supply it. We have the tendency to think, *Well, if I had what he or she has, I could serve also.* No, you can serve right where you are with what you have, and you can do it better than anyone else. God, in His love, has equipped you with everything you need to be successful.

I think of my wife. About fifty years ago, she adopted a son, Scott, who turned out to be a true hyperkinetic child. When her first husband died, she was forced to remove him from their home because he would have destroyed her and her three daughters. Scott wound up in a group home. One Sunday, Scott called my wife to tell her he had gotten saved. Thank God for the Baptists and their school buses, because one of them had picked up Scott and some others and taken them to church, where he met Jesus. This happened before we got married, and my wife had also recently gotten saved. She and Scott had a long conversation about it. Her task in this even though she, for the majority of the time represented in this story, was not a Christian, was to follow around this hyperkinetic child dealing with all the disasters. If you have never encountered a true hyperkinetic child, you have no idea what this means. And then, with the death of her husband, she was forced to allow children's services to remove Scott and place him. This went against every motherly instinct, but she finally realized that her love for Scott and her love for her three daughters required it.

A few years later, Scott died of an overdose. We were married by then and questioned the Children's Home Society about Scott's background. We were told that they believed he was a drug baby. Back then, little was known about drug babies. The prevalent thought was that once the babies were free of the addiction they were born with, they would be fine. Well, the years have proven otherwise, because a disproportionate number of drug babies have gone out the same way they came in.

I watched my wife bury her son, and I can tell you no parent should have to go through that. At Scott's funeral, the pastor spoke of Scott's personal relationship with Jesus and said he was now at home with Him forever. The morning after the funeral, my wife's mother asked her about the personal relationship Pastor Rayburn had mentioned. What did that mean? She had dreamt about it but did not understand what it was all about.

My wife and I explained that Scott had asked Jesus into his heart and had a personal relationship with Jesus as a result. We got a blank stare in response. I asked Frieda, my mother-in-law, if she knew the president of the United States, to which she said she knew who he was. I then asked if he knew her, and to that, she responded no. I asked why, and she stated they had never met. I explained, "So it is with you and Jesus. You know who He is, but He does not know you." My wife and I had the opportunity to introduce her seventy-nine-year-old mother to Jesus that morning. Without the pain of burying her grandchild, Frieda might never have met Jesus. This is the only time in my life that I have seen the pain and reason for something occur almost simultaneously. However,

What Is God's Planned Result?

God does generally work through pain. Had my wife not done what she did or had done it differently, the outcome could have been a disaster.

Third, God gives us the Holy Spirit to assist us in accomplishing our tasks. The Holy Spirit is forever with us, waiting for us to invite Him along. He is always on call to support us in whatever we are asked to do and is infinitely qualified to do His job. We are part of an intricate divine plan God developed at the beginning of creation to accomplish His divine purpose. I do not know what that purpose is, and even if I did, I probably would not understand it, let alone be able to explain it. But what I do know is that for whatever reason, He chose to use mankind to accomplish that purpose.

In Matthew 13:58, Matthew, in reflecting on a visit to Jesus' hometown, states that Jesus could not work many miracles there because of their unbelief. It is incredible to think that God, who has absolute control of the universe, chose one of the most unreliable things in His creation to accomplish His purpose – mankind. Also the passage states that our faith can accomplish things and the lack of it can prevent good things from happening.

I think it useful to once again think about something we all dread—trials and difficulties. James 1:2 (emphasis added) states, "Consider it all *joy*, my brothers, whenever you face trials of many kinds, because you know that the testing of your faith develops perseverance." If ever there was a statement that goes completely contrary to human thinking, that is it.

What, in a trial, is supposed to bring us joy? The first thing that comes to my mind is that God has enough faith in me to believe I will make it through the test successfully, and at the end, I will have learned what I need to learn. The fact that I am being tested is proof positive that God has selected me to do something for Him. I do not know about you, but knowing that the God of the universe needs me to do something for Him is mind-boggling.

God needs me to accomplish something. To me, that is an incredible statement, but the Bible is clear that nothing will be accomplished on this earth except through human agency. Whether human agency actually accomplishes the task or merely makes it possible, it is human agency that accomplishes anything that gets done. That is quite unbelievable if you spend time thinking about it.

Let's think of this in simple terms. In 2 Timothy 1, Paul states that before the world began, God saved us and called us to a holy life. As we have observed, that holy life is not automatic; we must work at it in order to accomplish it. That means we will often go through difficult and trying times as God attempts to mold us into useful vessels.

As discussed earlier, in John 15:1–8, Jesus speaks about being the vine while we are the branches. God prunes the fruitful branches to make them more fruitful, while the useless ones are cut off and thrown into the fire. It generally is not pleasant to have parts of our lives cut off and cast aside. Those parts can be friends who are bad for us, undesirable parts of our personalities, worldly possessions, bad habits, hobbies, or any number of other things that make up our lives. We may experience tremendous pain in losing something that has been an important part of our lives. We may have clung to it for a good period of time, and the loss of it threatens our identity and security. But think of this: the vinedresser is closest to the vine when he is inspecting it to see what needs to be removed in order to improve the health and increase the capacity for producing fruit.

So, what is the purpose of all this? God drew us out of our sinful state and provided us with the opportunity to accomplish something for Him. Think of that for a minute. God, the creator of the entire universe, the God who can do anything with nothing more than a spoken word, has called us to contribute something in the accomplishing of His divine purpose. Consider it in these terms. What if some famous person whom you have admired for a very long time knocked on your door and asked you to do something that he had determined no one else on the face of the earth was more qualified to do? How would that make you feel? Well, the God of the universe is knocking on your door and asking you to do something that no one else on the face of the earth

What Is God's Planned Result?

is more qualified to do. Not only is He asking you for your help, but He is giving you a Helper with infinite divine powers to walk by your side and assist you. Furthermore, not only is He giving you that assistant, but He is providing you with every possible tool and all the knowledge necessary to do it. And after you do it, He is storing up an eternal reward for your faithfulness.

God has had a divine plan in the works since before Genesis 1:1. When He developed His plan, He had a part in it for every believer.

Was it the same Jesus who did miracles everywhere He went, healing the sick, restoring sight to the blind, healing cripples, and performing many other miracles as He traveled? Yes. So why couldn't He work those miracles in His hometown? Because the townspeople did not have the faith. What is not getting done on earth because of our unbelief? What rewards will we miss out on because we did not believe God in something and, therefore, just let it go?

Part of God's plan is for us to pray; in fact, there are those whose entire ministry is prayer. Nevertheless, we all are called to pray. If we really believed in a miraculous God, wouldn't we pray more? We all are called to spread the gospel, but it seems to be one of the most difficult things for the average Christian to do. Is it possible some people will miss out on heaven because of our hesitancy to speak to them about Jesus? To me, that is a scary thought.

So, what is God's love language? God's love language is simply that He gives us an opportunity to perform our job in His intricate divine plan. He provides us with everything we need to do that job, and He protects us as we do it. If that job requires us to go through difficult, painful times, He is right there with us. The job may even require the giving of our lives; in that case, I cannot help but believe God would be with us in a manner we cannot even imagine.

In real, practical terms, God is all but doing our job, but we receive an eternal reward for having the faith to show up. The more I think about it, the more excited I get, especially since the average Christian need do nothing more than change their attitude in daily life. A good example is the flight attendant who stated she did not work for the airline, but for Jesus.

In reality, the large majority of Christians will not go into full-time service. If there were nothing but preachers, where would the congregations come from? If there were nothing but missionaries, where would their support come from? The majority of Christians will be called to live ordinary lives in an extraordinary way. They will be involved in God's service in what we might consider small ways, such as taking the time to pray for someone's situation, giving sacrificially when the church or some other ministry needs financial help, or taking care of widows and orphans in a practical way.

I am not advocating that every Christian become involved in every ministry that crosses their path; God has a way of making known what He wants us to do. For example, the children's ministry at my church is always looking for people to help them. I just say "thank you, but no thanks" because serving children is a fine and necessary ministry, but not mine. I did not like children when I was one. No matter who you are, there are ministries you are suited for and ministries you are not. Get involved with the ones you are suited for and avoid the others.

Recently I was helping a missionary from Australia with a car problem. As I was working on the vehicle, the woman mentioned a sermon she had heard a long time ago titled "Are You Willing to Live Your Entire Life to Accomplish a Ten-Minute Job for God?" That is an interesting question, and noteworthy. We have looked at the widow who put two small coins into the offering plate. She lived her entire life for that one moment.

Think of how different the world would look if every Christian were to suddenly live in the mindset that they needed to prepare for a ten-minute job in God's service somewhere down the road.

To close the book, lets condense God's love as much as possible. If you read the Bible, cover to cover, one of the central themes is that God loves us always. When we think of love our minds usually run to, I am giving this to you because I love you. But as a parent to a child, it can

What Is God's Planned Result?

often go to because I love you, I *will not let you have this.* Our minds generally gravitate to the former but God's mind seems to gravitate to the latter. God's first evidence of love is that he will not leave us where he found us. He will do everything in his power to encourage us to improve. Once he has our attention, He will begin teaching and guiding us to become whatever it is that He needs us to be to accomplish what he needs us to do. Any parent understands the concept of parental love and doing whatever it takes to mold a child into a responsible adult. Third, God has given all Christians access to the power and knowledge of the Holy Spirit. We always have the option of going to the Spirit for wisdom, strength, courage, and whatever else necessary to accomplish our task. And then he makes a generous deposit in our retirement account. Does this mean that God has no concern for our physical comfort? Absolutely not. Paul, by all accounts from a purely physical viewpoint, had a miserable life, but reading what he wrote he seemed to love every minute of it.

Listen to Christian radio. There are countless examples of people in various ministries, giving up physical pleasures to accomplish some heavenly purpose, and they would not change a thing. God will always give you what you need but he will not always give you what you want. He will however help you to be as comfortable as possible in whatever situation you are facing, provided that you are in the proper relationship with him.

Then there is the average Joe, the life of the vast majority of Christians. Getting up in the morning going to work doing whatever they do but doing it with the mind and attitude of Jesus, like the flight attendant. No stress, no disappointment, no worry about tomorrow, no concern about the outcome, just believing that God is in control. Just think about being able to enjoy your spouse, children, house, weekends, and anything else that comes to mind without the stress and worry. Yes, this is definitely possible by living a life with God as your primary concern. We have noted it before, you worry about God and let him worry about you. God has a lot more resources, knowledge, and power to address your concerns if you will let him.

GOD'S *Love* LANGUAGE

God wants to take your earthly journey with you. To help you with whatever problems and trials you may have. To rejoice with you in the moments of success and to give you a heavenly hug in the moments of failure. He very much wants to give you the opportunity to do something for him and, at the end, to take you home to a reward that is literally indescribable. No wonder Paul said I long to depart and be with Christ, but it is more heedful that I remain with you.

This is God's Love Language.

EPILOGUE

In the writing of this book, I began to think about heaven. I considered different scenarios. The first was Revelation 7:17, where the Bible says the Lamb at the center of the throne will be our shepherd; He will lead us to springs of living water. God also will wipe away every tear from our eyes. What are these tears in heaven? Where do they come from?

I can't help but wonder if one possibility is what Paul speaks of in 2 Corinthians 3:10–15, where he describes those who built with wood, hay, and stubble. When their work was tried in the fire, it was burned up, though they were saved as one coming through the fire. When these people realize they wasted their entire lives, and the chance of doing something for God has disappeared forever, will they break into tears, at which point God the Father will comfort them?

Another mental picture I thought of was people gathering for a chat. Someone in the group – let's say "Sam" – mentions a situation that radically changed his life. "Martha" speaks up to say she was the one in that situation but never gave it much thought because it seemed so insignificant. Sam answers that his life was radically changed by it and that he was prompted to completely redirect his life into a direction and location he had never considered before. Then "Carla" speaks up to say that because she encountered Sam, who was directed to her location by Martha, a whole host of circumstances took place that would not have occurred otherwise. Many more people chime in, recounting the events in their lives that resulted from this chain of events, and the blessings that resulted. Finally, the whole crowd spontaneously erupts in loud praise to God as they begin to understand the intricacies of the divine plan that was at work in their lives.

I don't know about you, but I want to be a part of a heavenly conversation someday. I want to reflect on the things God used me for and how some of them had some really dramatic results. And I want to remember, because of God's love, He allowed me to be part of it. I look forward to having conversations with others about their lives and rejoicing with them about the things that their lives affected. I do not know how much of eternity it will take to begin to unravel all the unknowns of different people's lives and the unknown things that happened because of what they did, but I am looking forward to every moment.

I encourage you to join me and many others in that conversation. Your heavenly 401(k) account is open and available for deposits, if you will just say "Okay."

And I am looking forward to having that conversation with *you* some day.

Lightning Source UK Ltd.
Milton Keynes UK
UKHW021629020720
365920UK00003B/333